GW01550928

Church and State
in Postwar Eastern Europe

RECENT TITLES IN
BIBLIOGRAPHIES AND INDEXES IN RELIGIOUS STUDIES

Theological and Religious Reference Materials: General Resources
and Biblical Studies
G. E. Gorman and Lyn Gorman, with the assistance of Donald N. Matthews

Theological and Religious Reference Materials: Systematic Theology
and Church History
G. E. Gorman and Lyn Gorman, with the assistance of Donald N. Matthews

Healing Faith: An Annotated Bibliography of Christian Self-Help Books
Elise Chase, compiler

New Religious Movements in the United States and Canada
Diane Choquette, compiler

Bibliography of Published Articles on American Presbyterianism, 1901-1980
Harold M. Parker, Jr., compiler

Contemporary Jewish Ethics: A Bibliographical Survey
S. Daniel Breslauer, compiler

Theological and Religious Reference Materials: Practical Theology
G. E. Gorman and Lyn Gorman, with the assistance of Donald N. Matthews

Modern Jewish Morality: A Bibliographical Survey
S. Daniel Breslauer, compiler

The Sociology of Religion: A Bibliographical Survey
Roger Homan, compiler

Black Theology:
A Critical Assessment and Annotated Bibliography
James H. Evans, Jr., compiler

Church and State in Postwar Eastern Europe

A Bibliographical Survey

Compiled by Paul Mojzes
G.E. Gorman, Advisory Editor

Bibliographies and Indexes in Religious Studies, Number 11

GREENWOOD PRESS
New York • Westport, Connecticut • London

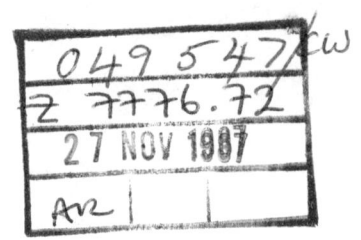

Library of Congress Cataloging-in-Publication Data

Church and state in postwar eastern Europe.

(Bibliographies and indexes in religious studies,
ISSN 0742-6836 ; no. 11)
  Bibliography: p.
  Includes index.
  1. Church and state—Europe, Eastern—History—20th
century—Bibliography. 2. Church and state—Communist
countries—History—20th century—Bibliography.
3. Persecution—Europe, Eastern—History—20th century—
Bibliography. 4. Persecution—Communist countries—
History—20th century—Bibliography. 5. Communism and
Christianity—Europe, Eastern—Bibliography.
6. Communism and Christianity—Communist countries—
Bibliography. 7. Europe, Eastern—Church history—
Bibliography. 8. Communist countries—Church history—
Bibliography. I. Mojzes, Paul. II. Gorman, G. E.
Z7776.72.C5   1987   016.322'1'0947   87-8358
[BR738.6]
ISBN 0-313-24002-7 (lib. bdg. : alk. paper)

Copyright © 1987 by Paul Mojzes

All rights reserved. No portion of this book may be
reproduced, by any process or technique, without the
express written consent of the publisher.

Library of Congress Catalog Card Number: 87-8358
ISBN: 0-313-24002-7
ISSN: 0742-6836

First published in 1987

Greenwood Press, Inc.
88 Post Road West, Westport, Connecticut 06881

Printed in the United States of America

The paper used in this book complies with the
Permanent Paper Standard issued by the National
Information Standards Organization (Z39.48-1984).

10 9 8 7 6 5 4 3 2 1

Dedicated to the many individuals in the Soviet Union and Eastern Europe who have agonized during tumultuous change in relationships between the churches and society seeking to humanize the process with integrity and courage of conviction.

Contents

PREFACE..IX

INTRODUCTORY SURVEY.......................................3

I. IMPACT OF THE EASTERN EUROPEAN CHURCHES ON SOCIETY......3
       NEW MODELS FOR THE CHURCHES........................5
       ATTITUDES OF THE CHURCHES TOWARD SOCIALISM.........8
       AREAS OF GREATEST IMPACT..........................12
       SOURCE OF THE CHURCHES' INFLUENCE.................17

II. IMPACT OF THE SOCIETY ON THE CHURCHES.................19
       THE SOVIET MODEL..................................20
       OTHER EASTERN EUROPEAN COUNTRIES..................21
       FACTORS INFLUENCING RELIGIOUS POLICY..............23

BIBLIOGRAPHICAL SURVEY....................................27

AREA-WIDE...27

INDIVIDUAL COUNTRIES......................................35
       UNION OF SOVIET SOCIALIST REPUBLICS...............35
           GENERAL.....................................35
           RUSSIAN ORTHODOX CHURCH.....................46
           EASTERN APOSTOLIC CHURCHES..................51
           ROMAN CATHOLIC CHURCH.......................51
           PROTESTANTS.................................54
       ALBANIA...57
       BULGARIA..58
       CZECHOSLOVAKIA....................................60
       EAST GERMANY......................................63
       HUNGARY...67
       POLAND..73
       ROMANIA...78
       YUGOSLAVIA..81

MISCELLANEOUS ISSUES......................................86
       CHRISTIAN PEACE CONFERENCE........................86
       JOURNALS..87

AUTHOR INDEX..91

TITLE INDEX...96

SUBJECT INDEX..106

Preface

Conditions surrounding the most traumatic assault which the Christian Church has experienced in its twenty centuries of existence, that of the encounter with Communism in the Soviet Union and Eastern Europe, are not conducive to extensive literary investigation, especially not of the scholarly kind. Most of those who were instrumental in inflicting this trauma have little desire to allow extensive investigation of the relationships between the societies which they control and the churches. Thus a body of literature arose that is often characterized by propaganda, half-truths, exaggeration, animosity, pain, manipulation and other aspects that make the discovery of truth difficult. But careful, balanced works are not entirely missing.

The subject of this annotated bibliography is the literature on the relationship between Soviet and Eastern European churches and the societies in which they have existed since the end of World War II. The chronological starting point of this period, 1945, is a natural one because countries that are now known by the politico-geographic designation of Eastern Europe (Albania, Bulgaria, Czechoslovakia, East Germany, Hungary, Poland, Romania, and Yugoslavia) came under Communist control either immediately following World War II or shortly thereafter. In the Soviet Union, the end of this war brought about a new form of relationship between the state and churches, so that there, too, this starting point is justified.

In order to shed some light on the mutual relations between the churches and society, two survey chapters are provided for the reader which may be of help in getting an orientation toward the subject matter for a more effective use of the existing bibliography. My attempt has been to write a judicious, balanced survey which might help the reader to discern in the literature those books that are either overtly slanted toward a propagandistic cover-up of the huge problems or reveal a belicose animosity toward all changes in the pre-war status of the churches by emphasizing only the persecution and oppression. In this case the truth does not lie somewhere in between, but, depending on a given country or a given period, the relations may be either entirely antagonistic and completely oppressive or relatively tolerant and livable.

The pattern of this book is simple. A two-part introductory survey provides an analytical context for the bibliography and indicates the most important literature. First, the attitude of the churches toward their society is analyzed; then, the reverse is attempted, with a description of the societal attitudes toward the churches. The bibliographical section first presents books and articles dealing with the entire region, after which entries appear within a country by country classification. Not surprisingly, the sources dealing with the USSR are most numerous. This is due not only because of the sheer size of that country and its pioneering dominance in matters communist, but also because of the Western fascination with this superpower and its particularly belligerent antireligious policy which other Eastern European states seek to emulate. The size of the Soviet bibliography led to its subdivision into materials dealing with (1) general and inclusive religious policies and issues, (2) the Russian Orthodox Church, (3) the Oriental Apostolic Churches (Georgian and Armenian), (4) the Roman Catholic Church, and (5) the Protestants and "sectarians." With other countries, such a division did not appear necessary or possible either because of the religious makeup of that country or the limited bibliography. It should be specifically mentioned that of the religions in Eastern Europe only the Christian is included here; Jewish, Muslim, and Buddhist related bibliography was not within the scope of this study. Another self-imposed limit was to cover only English literature or translations.

The bibliographical survey is neither fully comprehensive nor fully critically annotated. Brief reports on the situation of churches in denominational and popular magazines are both too numerous to include and too sketchy to be of use to the systematic collector or scholar. Other items were not readily available for examination, but were included anyway because I thought it useful to make the reader aware of their existence. In some instances certain publishing data is missing from such indirectly obtained references. Nevertheless, it is my conviction that the most important literature on the subject has been annotated, hopefully in a manner helpful to those needing to make decisions on book acquisitions. Author, title, and subject indexes conclude this work.

All bibliographical entries are enumerated for ease of access through the indexes and cross referencing. References to entry numbers of pertinent sources appear parenthetically within the introductory survey, and annotations of many items in the bibliographical survey end with reference to entry numbers of related items. The author, title, and subject indexes, which conclude the work, refer to page numbers in the introductory survey and item numbers in the bibliographical survey.

A brief clarification is needed about the use of capital and lower case letters in words like "church" and "communist." When caps are used, the reference is either to the Christian Church as a conceptual notion or to specific denominations, while the lower case is used when referring to a church building or to any nonspecified church. A similar principle is used with the term "communist." When a specific communist party is mentioned it is capitalized, while lower case is used when the reference is to the general communist movement or idea.

The Reverend Gary Gorman of Riverina-Murray Institute of Higher Education in Australia, Advisory Editor of this bibliographic series, who asked me to compile this book, rendered helpful guidance and made numerous suggestions on the writing of this book. He went beyond the normal tasks of series adviser by bringing more accuracy and elegance to the writing of a person to whom English is not the native tongue. Marilyn Brownstein of Greenwood Press also provided stylistic directions. My greatest indebtedness goes to Brian and Karen Rotz of West Chester, PA., who patiently and conscientiously transcribed my written notes onto a word processor and who are responsible for the appearance of the book. I also wish to thank the Connelly Fund of Rosemont College for financing the typing of the manuscript.

Church and State
in Postwar Eastern Europe

Introductory Survey

I. IMPACT OF THE EASTERN EUROPEAN CHURCHES ON SOCIETY

Had the Marxist forecasts regarding religion that were made at the time of Communist revolutions or takeovers in Eastern Europe been on target, one would have expected that the impact of the churches on society in the 1980s would be nil or at least so negligible as to negate the value or the possibility of a book on this subject. But they were wrong about the "withering away of religion," to borrow a Marxian phrase. Similarly incorrect were those opponents of Marxism who gloomily made the same predictions when they witnessed the massive Communist onslaught upon the churches and the ensuing suffering and destruction. The reality of the Eastern European religious situation is very different from that predicted, and it is much more variable than most casual observers and less careful students of the scene seem to discern.

Because of different historical circumstances, traditions, church policies and politics, as well as Communist party strengths or weaknesses in the application of Marxist precepts to religion and society, there is today an almost bewildering variety of ways in which the impact of the church is felt in the Soviet Union, Poland, East Germany, Czechoslovakia, Hungary, Romania, Yugoslavia, Bulgaria and Albania.

The Communist revolution brought the greatest challenge to organized religion since Christianity had received legal recognition under Constantine the Great early in the fourth century. There had been other great upheavals, starting with the brief restoration of "paganism" under Julian, a cousin of Constantine the Great, emperor from 361-363. There followed great and often violent rivalry between Christians and Jews, between Eastern Orthodox and Roman Catholics, and later in the sixteenth century between Catholics and Protestants. The Mongol and Turkish Muslim dominations also caused incalculable upheavals in the Christian communities of Russia and the Balkans. Prior to the Bolshevik revolution in 1917 and the immediate post-World War II period when the rest of Eastern Europe became socialist, religious institutions, particularly the large established churches, usually had a privileged status in the community and frequently exercised a dominant role in society. Among Christians this is called the Constantinian model of church-state relations in which the privileged church supports the social arrangement, which in turn guarantees it favored treatment.

It is easy to oversimplify the Constantinian model and present a situation where a particular church exerts such an influence that it runs the society and seeks for a monopoly at the expense of other potentially rival religions. Thus, not all churches and religious institutions found themselves in the Constantinian situation. Jews, for instance, never enjoyed such favored treatment and were only occasionally fortunate enough to find various degrees of tolerance. The same was true of the Protestant "sectarians" or so-called "Free Churches" (Baptists, Methodists, Mennonites, Pentecostals, Adventists), who sometimes experienced severe repression at the hands of established state churches and were frequently denied legal status. (For example, the Methodists obtained legal status in Poland only in 1945.) The pattern itself is not fully accurate, because during certain historical periods the state exercised a paramount influence over the church, as at the time of Peter the Great and his successors in Russia, who sought to reduce the Russian Orthodox Church to a convenient department of state and strictly controlled church activities. Nevertheless, many religious institutions enjoyed a status that granted them a great deal of power, influence, and prestige in society. In fact, the relationship between church and society tended to be so close that in many places there was an almost total identification of ethnicity with religious affiliation. Thus, Bulgarians, Romanians, Serbians, Macedonians, Montenegrins, Russians, and at times Ukrainians and White Russians were automatically, by birth, Orthodox. Croatians, Slovenes, Poles, and for all practical purposes the majority of Hungarians, Czechs, Slovaks, and Lithuanians were Roman Catholic, while East Germans were Protestants. Only in Hungary and among the Czechs and Slovaks were there also Protestants and some Orthodox who were not alienated from their ethnicity by belonging to a different religious tradition. Among Albanians there were Orthodox, Catholics and Muslims. It is hard for a person from outside the region to appreciate this extremely close identification of church with the nation -- an identification which, to this day, plays a very significant role and accounts for part of the impact that many churches continue to have (see 389). As one of the central and persistent factors of religious influence in Eastern Europe, it must not be neglected in any analysis.

When the Communists came to power, they generally attempted to implement a Leninist formula, only partially inspired by Marx, of legally separating the state and the schools from religion -- the American model of separation of church and state had little influence in Eastern Europe prior to the Communist rule -- and allowing limited legal existence to nearly all religious communities. From the perspective of the Communist party, religion is a reactionary reflection of former class societies which stands in the way of progress and must be combatted by all available means short of creating a boomerang effect of intensifying religious fervor. Since the Communist party exercises, in Marxist parlance, "the leading role" in the state, these two theoretically different approaches coalesced in reality into a single practice of massive state intervention in religious matters seeking to restrict and ultimately abolish institutional religion. The implementation of such policy depended on the resiliency of the religious communities and the needs of the state (see 043). For instance, Stalin needed the support of the Russian Orthodox Church during the Nazi offensive, so he relaxed some pressures and gave permission for the partial rebuilding of the ecclesiastical hierarchy (See 052, 119, 123, 151, 158, 160). Similarly, the churches' aid might be sought in implementation of certain agricultural policies to induce the population to work harder. This is done in exchange for certain privileges to the church. The Communist Party tacitly concedes that the church has influence among certain groups of the population where the party's influence is small.

New Models for the Churches

It is understood by the Communist parties, as well as by the churches, that the ultimate Communist aim is a society in which no organized religion will exist or exert any influence (109, 124). This pressure presents a radically new situation which different churches have dealt with in various ways. For none of the churches was the new situation totally welcomed; however, they have learned to adjust one way or another, and some have even come to praise it. This radically new position of the churches in the fully *etatized* society means that secular and religious authorities are in conflict, that in the process those churches which previously had political power have lost it. In some instances, however, the church has become recognized as the "principal moral authority," giving it "a new source of strength" (325).

The best example of the new situation in which a church has maintained or perhaps even gained additional social power is the Polish Roman Catholic Church (322, 325, 326). The model this church has selected is that of a firm pastoral caretaker of the Polish people, which sometimes leads it to support certain government measures but which also brings it into conflict with the government, e.g. on "Solidarity" (340, pp. 3-25). The Polish Roman Catholic Church avoids an explicitly political role. It claims its historical, legal, and religious right to speak out in defense of the Polish people, their society, and the human rights of individuals and groups. Since the Roman Catholic Church historically has been identified with the interests of the Polish people, and since nearly all Poles acknowledge themselves to be Roman Catholic in a manner resembling the medieval synthesis of religion with general life, the Church has been considered as a defender of the people (including the working class) against an alien, Soviet-imposed ideology. The Catholic Church in Poland thus feels free to enter into discussions and negotiations with the government as a legitimate defender of the welfare of the people (019, 347). The Polish United Workers' Party has apparently recognized that it cannot rule Poland without at least tacit, though qualified, approval from the Church.

In contrast to the Polish model, the Hungarian Roman Catholic Church and József Cardinal Mindszenty (304, 305 306, 316) stood in total opposition to the new Communist government from the post-war years to the mid-1960s (286, pp 19-23). Here the church was perceived mainly as the defender of its former rights and accepted the government challenge to a fight to the end. Such a posture could not be maintained indefinitely (285, 286, 287, 290), though such opposition could resurface in time of crisis against any Communist regime. This model seems now to have vanished.

Other Eastern European Church leaders, who likewise realized the disappearance of the Constantinian model, have promoted a third model for the churches. The theologians of the Church of the Czech Brethren, inspired by their famous and controversial theologian, Joseph Hromádka (1889-1969), said the church should welcome the new socialist order and become a "pilgrim church" representing the crucified Christ to the world, eschewing political power but seeking to transform and help the Communists, whom Hromadka saw as radical transformers of exploitive and unjust class societies (238, 244, 250). In Hromádka's opinion, the church should provide overall support to the new order, generally saying "yes," but saying a decisive "no" when it is obvious that major decisions are evil. In practice his followers generally justified and supported most government policies. Hromádka himself had a chance to voice a decisive "no" when the Soviets and their allies invaded Czechoslovakia in 1968 (244). He died soon thereafter. Hromádka's influence was decisive in Czechoslovakia and quite strong among Hungarian and East German Protestants.

The Hungarian Protestants coined the phrase, "the servant Church," and promoted a "theology of diaconia," which is a variant of the model of the Church of the Czech Brethren. Their leaders stress service to society and show an ardent desire to make accommodations with the government (293). Many of their theologians see the demolition of the Constantinian model as a distinct blessing for the church, an opportunity to get back to the real task of the church, namely not to rule but to serve (019). The early apostolic church is deemed worth emulating. Some people, however, have wondered whether the leadership of the Hungarian Reformed and Lutheran Churches has not become so subvervient that it simply seeks uncritically to implement government policies (314, 315). The leadership of the Hungarian Protestant churches may feel that there is no reason to raise the prophetic voice at home (though it directs prophetic messages to the West), since matters have been gradually improving during the Kadar regime. Protestant leaders feel that their policy has yielded results in the general improvement of conditions in society and for the churches (313). This model seems to have brought about the greatest cooperation of the churches with the postwar regime (303). The model is also being followed, perhaps with even greater enthusiasm, by a small number of Christians who are members of the Christian Democratic Union in East Germany; they see themselves as transmitters of decisions of the Socialist Unity Party to the Christian populace (273).

However, most Christians in East Germany have followed a different path of critical cooperation (013). They have sought to establish a **modus vivendi** within the socialist system by offering a distinctive Christian contribution to their people and retaining a certain critical distance from the government (251, 258, 259, 268, 270, 272). Generally, there is little ideological dialogue between church leadership and theologians on one hand the party on the other, but Christians stress limited cooperation and the attempt to work out an authentic Christian contribution to the new socialist environment (005, pp. 167-189).

The Eastern Orthodox Churches, deeply steeped in liturgical tradition, have embraced none of these models (019). Their main concern is to continue to offer the salvific mysteries to their people with the conviction that God shall not allow the Church to perish (038). Empires come and empires go, some friendly, others antagonistic, but the Church of Christ will last eternally. Their policy of acquiescence or patriotic endorsement of the policies of their nation bothers many Western activists, but it stems from a long experience that survival demands flexibility, silence in the political arena during years of persecution, and a dogged determination to provide liturgical opportunities and preserve the canonical structures of the church. Many of their leaders have suffered harsh persecution but the Orthodox believe that God's domain includes the entire nation, even those who persecute them. The Russian Orthodox Church (closely followed by the Bulgarian Orthodox Church) has undoubtedly faced the most antagonistic environment since 1917 and has come formally to endorse and praise the Soviet regime as the price for being allowed a limited sphere of activity. The other Orthodox Churches show more autonomy in regard to the government, but in each case they seek a very close identification with the people. While the degree of endorsement of official policies differs among prelates and people, it is fair to say that underneath it all the Orthodox Churches do not prefer socialism.

Still another model is being embraced by many "sectarians," those belonging to the small religious communities. Dominated generally by an apocalyptic pietistic theology (212, pp. 337-355), their perception is that this world is quickly approaching its end and the power of evil is making its last convulsive efforts to dominate this world. Some identify Communism as this power of evil; others regard all secular government as equally inimical to God's plans. Soon God will be victorious, and all the faithful will be saved eternally, while those opposing God's reign will be damned. Their emphasis is on personal salvation with little or no interest in making a public impact. They often gain adherents from marginal segments of society, as is evident among the Evangelical Baptists in the USSR and the Baptists of Romania, because their theology presents a sharp ideological alternative to official Marxist teaching which leaves many people untouched. Though their overall impact is generally small, they often find themselves in the limelight, as many of them heroically endure government harrassment, while bravely standing up for their rights. The dissenters, especially from among the "_initsiativniki_" or Reform

Evangelical Baptists, such as Georgiy Vinns, have become familiar to many in the West, epitomizing courageous struggle against those denying religious liberties (194). They are, however, not always perceived positively in their own countries, even among other Christians, some of whom consider them too fanatical, too sectarian, and hence exclusivistic and intolerant.

It should be emphasized that these models are rarely practiced uniformly and in their purity. Even within the churches that follow a particular model, there is a pluralism of approaches. The distinct histories and theologies of the various churches make it impossible for a church drastically to change its chosen model. The title of Trevor Beeson's Discretion and Valour (005) aptly summarizes the two most important options within the models, some choosing one path, some the other. A few church leaders opted for selling out altogether, e.g., János Péter, former bishop of the Hungarian Reformed Church (293), while others have chosen the path of hateful opposition, e.g., Richard Wurmbrand, formerly of Romania (380-385), and Haralan Popoff, formerly of Bulgaria (230-231); but the vast majority of Christians in Eastern Europe seek a constructive model in the difficult task of operating under socialist conditions.

Attitudes of the Churches Toward Socialism

The model of church activity is of intrinsic interest, but its importance is heightened by the fact that the Communist parties made an effort to eliminate all other political, social, intellectual, economic, and even sporting organizations which had any independence. The church remained de facto the only major institution that espoused an ideology other than Marxism. The Communists soon perceived that the churches might be used as an instrument of resistance against their mode of organizing society. The same insight occurred to those who wanted to show their disapproval of the established order; they would sometimes support the churches not for religious reasons but because they wanted to express an unfavorable attitude toward the government. When one adds to this the undeniable fact that there were very few Communist sympathizers among active church leaders, it becomes evident that the churches were, from the outset, counted among those who would oppose Communist policies. This posture can be labeled "religion against socialism" or even anti-socialist religion.

That "religion against socialism" is still the prevalent church attitude needs no documentation. The first years of Communist takeover were characterized by sometimes bitter and violent confrontation. The state resorted to repressive measures causing martyrdom and great devastation individually and institutionally.

Marxists judged the impact of religion upon social policies as altogether negative. For them the only question was what was the most effective way of confronting the churches. Tactical approaches differed. In some instances the major church in a country was attacked so mercilessly that smaller churches saw that resistance was fruitless and were cowed into silence. This was the case with the Catholic Church in Hungary (305, 306, 310), Czechoslovakia (242, 243) and Lithuania (178, 183, 189-193), where the most bitter resistance against the new socialist society came from Roman Catholics. In other instances the policy was to make an example of a smaller church, thus providing a lesson to the larger church to avoid confrontation. This occurred in Bulgaria, where the state targeted its attack on the four small Protestant churches and succeeded in intimidating the Bulgarian Orthodox Church (230, 233, 234). The dissenting Christians in the USSR often belong to this category (194, 196, 198, 212, 214).

The second possible posture is "religion indifferent to socialism." According to this approach, the life of the churches goes on without either showing active resistance or embracing the new social order (150, 154). This is usually a form of accommodation which considers all social orders as temporary in nature, while the church has an abiding sense of mission and will survive any social order as it did the Roman or Byzantine Empires and Turkish rule. Many Eastern Orthodox Churches have assumed this posture of tacit acquiescence coupled with the hope of divine deliverance. The church avoids any explicitly political posture, neither directly aiding nor resisting socialism. At best some church leaders declare from time to time that certain socialist policies are not inimical to church teachings or that they may be in accord with a long-held church position (for example, on curbing personal greed or trying to bring peace). The latter issue (working for peace) is by far the most mutually acceptable social issue on which a politically non involved church and the state can find a common platform (147-149). In most socialist societies the churches have been encouraged by the government to work for peace, as it was hoped that by careful influence the church's position could be made inoffensive or in tune with the government's foreign policy.

The third form of accommodation may be called "religion in socialism," or "religion within socialism." This phrase was coined by leaders of the Evangelical (Lutheran) Churches in East Germany as they struggled to find a theologically and socially productive relationship with socialism (251, 254, 268, 270, 276, 281). They rejected the former two models, which they felt created a mentality of being an alien in one's own land. Indeed, many East Germans were "spiritual emigrants," looking forward to German reunion to free them from the Soviet-type socialist imposition. Others in East Germany aggressively urged a much more intimate endorsement of socialism, a "religion for socialism" (described below). With the phrase, "the church within socialism," it was hoped to communicate acceptance of the fact that the social system for the forseeable future was socialist and that wishful thinking would not change it. Thus the church accepts as its mission to work in this particular socialist society without nurturing illusions about escape to the West or some magic disappearance of socialism (272, 279). The church has a task of humanizing and interacting with the system in whatever manner possible. With this approach it is possible for the churches in East Germany to maintain a number of its social and charitable institutions, such as hospitals, old people's homes, and youth fellowships; and occasionally the churches do speak out against certain social policies (for example, universal military conscription or pre-military education in the schools).

"Religion for socialism" is a minority approach among churches in Eastern Europe, but it has its adherents (269, 273). Their motivation and actions vary considerably. Some are simply opportunists or careerists, but others are theologically or socially sensitive people who were shocked by the church's reactionary policies of the past, when the church may have been an accomplice of pro-Nazi policies or sided with the privileged classes, giving no heed to the poor and downtrodden. In their opinion this past behavior requires total repentance. Socialism is seen either as an instrument of punishment by God or, more frequently, as God working outside the realm of the churches, even by means of a hostile, atheistic social system, to bring about greater social justice and harmony than existed in the previous social system. Many protagonists of "religion for socialism" perceive the world to be shaped through the struggle of two social systems-capitalism, which they see as on its way out, and socialism, which they believe to be the wave of the future. There is no third way, they say (029). Thus one must decide for socialism (East Germans call it "partisanship"), because socialism means progress, peace, justice, equality, and dignity. According to this view, sitting on the fence is as bad as being for capitalism. The first vigorously to espouse such views in Eastern Europe was the famous and controversial Czech theologian, Joseph Hromadka (238, 250), who swayed many young theologians in his church (the Czech Brethren) and outside to follow him on this path of bold acceptance of socialism with the attempt to gain credence in socialist society, so that eventually the church could serve it more effectively (241, 244).

The Hungarian Reformed bishop Albert Bereczky pioneered a similar approach in Hungary (293). He led the Reformed and Lutheran Churches, after some bitter inter-church battles, into a posture of officially giving their support, usually uncritically to the social system. This attitude earned certain privileges for church leaders who were deemed reliable by the government, including representation in the parliament (analogous to their role in pre-socialist times) or state payment of clerical salaries. But the price has been that this church leadership self-censored expressions of dissent (291, 298). The only time when either internal opposition to this course or popular resentment against such policiessurfaced was during the 1956 Hungarian Revolt. At that time nearly all the vocal proponents of "religion for socialism"were quickly demoted, only to be reinstated shortly afterthe crushing of the revolt (293).

There is also the group of younger clergy, born since the establishment of socialism, for whom socialism is the only social system they have experienced. For a number of them there is no feeling of guilt or sentimental wishing for the return of the past. While they accept as normal the life of the church under socialism, they also tend to be critical, not so much of the system per se, but of shortcomings in the implementation of socialist ideals. They are more likely to feel secure in questioning day-to-day policies. Usually they lack the zeal or idealistic enthusiasm of their older colleagues, yet they do not even contemplate what it would be like if socialism were not the system in their country. Many of them think that socialism has made some advances which should not be given up. If they oppose a particular issue, it usually does not mean that they oppose socialism as such. One can see such an attitude among the many youthful Christians who were involved in the upheavals in Hungary, Czechoslovakia, and Poland (321, 033).

It may come as a surprise to many that there is one more model, which we can loosely tag as "socialist religion." That should be a contradiction in terms, but it is not. Perceptive analysts noted long ago that Marxism may turn into a "pseudo-religion" for some adherents. Now even many Marxists recognize that one may have a "religious" attitude toward socialism. One Marxist wrote of "black clericalism" being supplanted by "red clericalism" or "atheist clericalism." While in most instances such "socialist religion" is evaluated negatively by both Marxist and non-Marxist thinkers, it is evident that socialism can elicit the kind of response which usually characterizes religious movements, though, in the opinion of many Christians, socialism is an idolatrous "religion." Therefore, one must use the category of "socialist religion" very carefully and in a nuanced way. It should be granted, however, that there is such a phenomenon as "socialist religion"; and that it is most developed among the socialist bureaucracy (aparatchiks). In this form religion continues to have a profound social impact under socialism (for example Stalinism, Maoism, or any other "cult of personality").

Not all churches can easily be categorized according to this typology. The Roman Catholic Church in Poland, which undoubtedly has the greatest social impact of all Eastern European churches, may be perceived by different people to fit different categories. Many have seen it as the staunchest social opponent of the Soviet-type socialism which is dominant in Poland (322, 325, 326, 341, 347). Its moral authority is derived from its unflinching protection of certain rights and ideals. Others attribute the success of the Polish Roman Catholic Church to its wisdom in not playing an overtly political role but in distancing itself from the socialist system. At the same time, the church passionately identifies with Polish national interests. Sometimes this produces policies in support of the governing party and sometimes advocacy of opposition. Finally some perceive the Polish Roman Catholic Church as having come to terms with life under socialism and pursuing a course of critical acceptance, embracing certain features of the new social reality but lashing out at others.

Currently the first three models are most widely utilized, though it is difficult to quantify this generalization; perhaps the largest number of religious people vaguely opt for the second model of "religion indifferent to socialism," as the least demanding and, under conditions of bureaucratic totalitarianism, the most favored by the system. The most creative option seems to be "religion within socialism," which is based on the presupposition that religion can operate in a variety of social systems and that it need not merely adapt itself to them but can engage critically in the process of social transformation, depending on political circumstances. This view holds that no given social system is inherently "Christian" but that the more fundamental issue is how any social system is made to serve basic human needs, including spiritual ones. The option "religion for socialism" likewise has produced some thoughtful, as well as some naive or sinister, theological reflections which value those features of socialism most in accord with humane religious objectives and promote their implementation instead of systems of injustice.

If one were to ask which of these models is most effective in influencing social policies, no clear answer can be given. It is not so much the model itself which determines influence, but a whole network of historical, national, political (foreign and domestic), economic, and other aspects. A church's intransigent opposition to socialism may either relegate it to obscurity or catapult it into the focus of opposition, depending on factors such as the power of the party, the success or failure of economic policies, international relations, national identification, etc. Should, for instance, the Yugoslav federation become politically jeopardized and Croatian separatism become a more potent movement, the Roman Catholic Church may be perceived as protector of Croatian national values and thus increase its influence. On the other hand should the federation succeed and the Catholic Church be unable to adjust to this reality, it may be relegated to the role of a minor nuisance on such issues as abortion laws. Much depends on a church's perceptive judgment of not only the political mood of the country but also what is ultimately right or wrong for the people it represents and for those it does not represent but cares for.

The only option doomed not to have long range social effects, in my view, is a non-critical supportive attitude. In the short run this policy may yield some practical results, for instance, in being able to intervene on behalf of individuals imprisoned or persecuted and in being able to soften the impact of this or that decree. However, in the long run a position which merely restates the views of policy makers is respected neither by the promoters (because one did not completely join them) nor by the critics or dissenters or even the passive part of the population, because they perceive the group as being compromised, as being "bought off" or duped. In any case a Christian who can say "yes" to a society can meaningfully do so only if she or he can also say "no." Merely saying "yes" does not make distinctions between God and Caesar. Potentially and actually, that is the core of the issue of the social impact of Christians in a society that tends to require absolute allegiance to Caesar. The very fact that Christians (and other religionists) do not share this allegiance makes religion both potentially and positively an autonomous source of social influence.

Areas of Greatest Impact

Now one may ask in what areas religion tends to show the greatest and most constant impact on public policy? In Eastern Europe, in addition to the traditional impact on ethnic or national policies, concern for the implementation of ethical or religio-ethical values has the greatest impact and is appreciated even by those rarely willing to praise religion.

When one considers the question of the relative power of Marxist ideology or religion or nationalism, nationalism appears to be the most potent force (034, 110, 347). While some people are ready to die for the Communist ideology, this cannot be said of the majority. Many people undoubtedly should be willing to make the supreme sacrifice in the name of their religion, but they are not in the majority either. Nationalism (and in multinational states, ethnicity of the component national units) is probably the most potent motivator for the largest number of people. The universal claims of religion and the internationalist claims of Communist ideology have had to make allowances for the influence of nationalism. Communists have realized that national Communism is a potent factor among socialist states and parties. The churches have long been willing to maintain a very close relationship with the nationality of their territory. Both church and state must cope with the impact of nationalism. Both have often sought to demonstrate their own loyalty to it and, likewise, have attempted to cast doubt on loyalty to the national idea on the part of their adversary. The government often finds itself at odds with a church's impact and attempts to counteract it, being quite aware of the potent effect that the churches can have in volatile nationalistic conflict situations. The policies of a church can either accentuate or diminish national enmity. The government is usually quite aware of the power of the church in this area and takes it into account in its legislative and administrative policies.

Religion also has an impact on social and individual ethical matters (241, 289). While this is an area in which churches have exerted influence over the centuries, in Eastern European socialist societies the ethical impact of the churches has been heightened due to two factors. One is that rapid industrialization and urbanization brought about almost total breakdown of the traditional interpersonal and social links which reinforced the norms and mores of the earlier era. This situation has left many people adrift. On the other hand, Marxism has not paid a great deal of attention to the development and inculcation of ethical norms despite frequent appeals to socialist morality. The predominant approach to ethics among Communists has been a pragmatic one that tended to relativize all norms subject only to the ultimate goal of Communist victory.

With large segments of the population set adrift and without constraints, many institutions suffered, including the family, economic enterprises, and the government itself. Low working morale, sabotage, laziness, theft, bribery, nepotism, lack of personal integrity and civil courage were among the results which harmed productivity and living standards. Marxist leaders noticed that religiously motivated people often resisted such temptations more effectively than others. They welcomed the church's appeals to members to uphold ethical norms, as the government would profit from their exhortations (282, 303). Thus, for instance, the government welcomed the endorsement of their agricultural policies of collectivization by the Hungarian Protestant churches. Peasants were urged to cooperate for the national welfare. The Roman Catholic bishops and clergy frequently appealed to a higher work ethic among Polish workers, being, however, careful to balance it with criticism of bureaucratic misdeeds (325, 336, 341). This is one of the reasons why the Catholic Church became so successful as a mediator between the government and the Solidarity labor union. In East Germany the Protestant churches appealed to young people and others to go to the farms and help with the harvest when the government requested such voluntary labor. But the government rejected the use of Christian labor brigades who set out to work in the fields and celebrated a shared communal meal interpreted by participants as Holy Communion.

Sometimes the churches' ethical teachings reflect only the traditional way of doing things and can be seen by the state as an obstacle to social change. Thus, for instance, certain cultural mores and superstitious practices that were associated with religion continue to be advocated by certain church members or leaders. These may be "faith healing" in preference to medical attention, avoidance of certain foods or rejection of public education. In an atheistic state where propaganda attempts to portray the conflict as a struggle between science and religion, it may be to the advantage of the government to caricature all religion as being associated with traditional superstitious folkways and values.

Sometimes the religio-ethical values of a church exist in opposition to intended government policies. This has been the case with the Roman Catholic Church concerning divorce laws, abortion, and birth control laws. The government maintains that this is involvement of the church in the political arena contrary to the principle of separation of church and state; the Church maintains that it is the protection of human rights. (One needs to mention, parenthetically, that Marxist convictions are often totally pragmatic: in Hungary a liberal abortion law was passed, only to be quickly rescinded when the birthrate was deemed insufficient.)

While some of the religious impact in the sphere of ethics occurs in conflict with Marxist notions, this is not always the case. There is room for dialogue and mutual influence or complementarity (029). Marxism has a more developed theory of work and its creative place in human development. On the other hand religion has tended to promote a responsible attitude toward work. In Poland, for instance, Christians and Marxists engaged in dialogue on the nature and dignity of work. Dialogue on ethical issues is only beginning, but if it were to be pursued, it could prove beneficial to both parties (289).

Another area for cooperation is the struggle for peace and disarmament. Without judging the genuineness of the Communist desire for peace, the proclaimed policy of Communist governments is peace with justice (on their terms, of course). The countries of Eastern Europe have been frequently involved in devastating wars culminating in World War II, yet the population genuinely desires peace. Therefore, it is not hard for the churches to recall that it is their task to strive for peace and justice. It is irrelevant that Communist governments may be using the churches for certain propaganda purposes; at least externally the goals seem to be parallel (154). While the churches rarely have had the freedom to take an explicitly critical attitude toward their own government's policies, at least in some instances church appeals were directed toward all governments to end the arms race and in particular to ban nuclear weapons (414, 416). Since conscription is universal in Eastern European countries, the churches have not endorsed pacifism, as they hasten to point out, and have not defended conscientious objection. The only exception is in East

Germany, where some young Christians have voiced their objections to performing military duties (252, 263, 264, 267). Some local churches and some church leaders have cautiously defended their young members. The fact that this disturbs the government probably is a greater testimony to the abnormal fear by the Communist government of any dissent than to the actual power of the church to alter state policies (252).

If being humane is of value to the churches, then the greatest influence they could have would be to bring a "human face" to socialism, as the Czechoslovaks stated in 1968 (241). Whether that is possible remains to be seen; previous failures do not preclude that possibility for all eternity. An investigation still needs to be made into whether contemporary forms of socialism are capable of becoming the kind of liberating societies that Marx dreamed of; but certainly some improvements are possible. In a few instances churches have consciously worked in that direction.

In societies in which the government attempts to deny pluralism, overstresses unity, and strives to have complete consensus on all issues, the churches have prevented full assimilation and uniformity. In the past it was easier for religions to identify themselves with social forms; but since Communism fosters an atheist society, such syncretism is extremely difficult (290). This guarantees at least some degree of diversity in a given country and is a very distinctive factor to policy makers, who experience this as a barrier to uniformity.

The influence of a new kind of spiritualism has been noted among intellectuals and the young in some places in Eastern Europe, notably in the Soviet Union as described by Alexander Solzhenitsyn (157) and Mihajlo Mihajlov. Its impact is not yet measurable, and is latent rather than actual (051). Another potential impact is that of popular religious leaders, such as the martyred Fr. Jerzy Popiełusko in Poland (344) or the startsi (ascetic, monastic old men living in seclusion but revered for their holiness by the masses) and certain bishops or the Pope (330, 349), who might, in a crisis, provide suitable leadership for dissenters. Especially in the rural areas, the population often accords great respect to clergy, in particular to higher clergy. In Romania, for instance, the bishops of the Orthodox Church may have an entire village, including the Communist officials, go out spontaneously to greet them upon arrival; such a welcome may not be accorded to government officials, even with considerable prior preparation. The Slavic term vladika (meaning "ruler") is still conventionally applied to many Orthodox bishops. A similar respect is enjoyed by Roman Catholic hierarchs. In Hungary some of the higher clergy are still members of Parliament. While this does not mean that they have outright political power, it does serve as a sign of recognition in their society. They are accorded V.I.P. status at receptions and airports and in the media.

In two of the Eastern European countries the religious press plays an independent and influential role. In Poland this press is particularly vigorous and has never been totally curtailed (319, 328). It publishes journals, magazines, and even weekly newspapers (for example, Więź and Tygodnik Powszechny). During liberal periods such a press becomes particularly active in providing alternative interpretations of events and issues. In Yugoslavia the religious press was nearly eliminated after the Communist take-over but was revived in the 1960s. Currently it is sufficiently independent to criticize the government, sometimes in veiled and sometimes in open ways. In response certain publications are occasionally banned. The religious press was also vigorous in Czechoslovakia during the "Prague Spring" but is now so tightly controlled that it has became inocuous. Hungarian, Romanian, and East German religious publications seem to have little political influence. The other countries, especially Albania and the USSR, have either a very limited religious press or none at all.

Two countries have church-affiliated political parties or organizations with political representation in parliament. In East Germany the Christian Democratic Union is guaranteed a fixed number of seats in the legislature. After World War II it conceived of itself as potentially independent but soon defined itself as a vehicle for implementing the "scientific" views of the ruling Socialist Unity Party (Marxist). Currently it is not providing any alternative options (273). However, leading personalities of this party often occupy important offices (for example, supreme court justice, president of the parliament). In Poland several Roman Catholic lay organizations, namely "Znak," "Pax" and the "Christian Social Association," have a designated number of their leaders (not more than five each) in the *Seym* (342). In some instances these deputies have abstained from voting for government policies. A few have even voted against the government, which has caused much agitation and sometimes replacement of the "errant" deputies. No such political groupings exist in other Eastern European countries.

Schools are another potential influence in society. For that reason a sharp separation of schools from the church was advocated by the Communists and carried out in Eastern Europe. Nearly all church schools became public. The exception, again, is Poland, where the Catholic University in Lublin is the only such private institution in Eastern Europe. There are two other academies which likewise train students not intending to be ordained as clergy. In other countries church schools are primarily theological seminaries or preparatory religious schools, though in Hungary a few high schools have been left in church hands.

It is common knowledge that there were no independent labor unions in Eastern Europe until the creation of Solidarity in Poland in 1980. The impact of the Roman Catholic Church on this independent union movement is fairly well known (336, 350). In this case the demands of the labor union leaders included more religious liberty, the use of mass media for communicating religious ceremonies and sermons, and frequent prayers and priestly counsel, such as consultation with the highest clergy and the primate of Poland. Solidarity has been the largest mass movement in Poland's history, and the Roman Catholic Church played a central role in this movement. One can regard this as the high watermark of political and social influence of a church in Eastern Europe under a Communist regime.

Source of the Churches' Influence

The churches are still the single largest mass organization in each Eastern European country, and this undoubtedly has contributed to their impact, although the Communist party has worked out a fairly effective domination of society as a minority movement.

Size is enhanced by the perception that religious institutions are among the very few independent bodies permitted to function in a Communist society. Thus, as noted above, churches sometimes draw the support of dissenters and other dissatisfied people. When, at an Easter midnight liturgy in Tbilisi, Georgia, in the early 1980's the church was crowded with young males between fifteen and thirty, that is probably less an expression of religious fervor and more a Georgian nationalistic demonstration against central government policies of Russification. If at the grave site of Alojzije Cardinal Stepinac in Zagreb thousands of people place flowers or candles, they were not merely coming to pay respect to a dead prelate but are making a statement about Croatian nationalism and defying the government which attempted to crush Stepinac. The crosses made of flowers in Warsaw in August 1982 were more a symbol of resistance to military rule than purely religious symbols. These examples of resistance took on distinct religious symbolism.

Another reason for the impact of religion is the power of tradition in a world that shows little appreciation for traditions. Religion appears to be one of the few stable elements in a rapidly changing world. Many are yearning for stability and security and are hoping to find it in institutions that have tended to embody such stability and have sought to preserve traditional values.

The churches have also tended to help individuals in time of need and have placed some emphasis on personal salvation. The bureaucratic totalitarianism that emerged in Eastern Europe as a result of the interaction of Marxist ideology and modern industrialization, urbanization, and secularization seems to show very little interest in the individual and his or her problems. Where will a person go when haunted by fear, doubt, anxiety, loneliness, rejection, loss of dignity and respect? Or where will a person celebrate the festive elements of life, such as birth, puberty, marriage, and death? To whom will one divulge a troubled conscience? Secular society has not provided enough avenues for personal concerns, and the churches have continued to fulfill an important function.

Many people feel the need for change or transformation, for they are not happy with themselves as they are. Perhaps they are adrift or unfulfilled. Unlike in the West, society in the East does not provide for such needs, because psychological counselling and analysis are not generally available. Many people have experienced the great transformational power of God in some aspect of church life to such a degree that they consider it the central experience of their lives. The result is that they give absolute allegiance to what is for them the ultimate source of all good. Thus other goals, such as class struggle, victory of the proletariat, leadership of the Communist party, or the great future society, always come under God's ultimate rule. Religious people have most effectively refused to raise the lesser values of life to the level of ultimacy. Their faith in God helps them to judge these lesser claims and keep their demands in a different perspective. This appears to be the very core of religion's influence. From the government's perspective this is a grave threat, because it seems to decrease loyalty on the part of a considerable number of citizens. Churches have consequently been accused of unpatriotic, traitorous behavior. This was the explicit charge in a number of show trials in the late 1940s and early 1950s (230, 242, 295, 296, 304-306, 403, 413). Roman Catholic and other churches with a strong foreign connection have been additionally accused of betraying the state to the Vatican, or the United States, or some other foreign power.

The churches have normally affirmed their loyalty of the state and thereby recognized the government as legitimate. Nevertheless, they have maintained that God's law has primacy over state law when the two are in conflict.

Since much Eastern European legislation discriminates against religion by prohibiting or restricting many traditional religious activities, many religious people do indeed perceive a conflict between their duty to God and their duty to the state. In times of intense crisis -- such as happened during 1956 in Hungary, 1968 in Czechoslovakia, and the 1980s in Poland -- for some religious people the tension becomes unbearable, and they turn against the government, actively or passively. In such circumstances, religion may directly turn against the state, which it is unlikely to do in more stable times.

From the above it is obvious that it is dangerous to generalize about the influence of the churches upon social policies of the Soviet Union and Eastern Europe. One should neither overemphasize nor underrate their influence. The role of the Catholic Church in Poland is not an accurate indication of the secular role of other churches; but, on the other hand, neither is the Russian Orthodox experience the best indicator. The impact varies from country to country and from church to church.

II. IMPACT OF THE SOCIETY ON THE CHURCHES

The determining role of the Communist parties in Eastern European society makes it both easier and more difficult to assess the impact that society has made upon churches since 1945. It is easier because the monopoly of the Communist party in deciding on social policies is so pronounced that studying the Marxist policies toward religion in a given country gives a clear picture of the situation. On the other hand, this is difficult because most members of society do not share the Marxist attitude toward religion and toward churches in general; yet they rarely, and in some countries never, have the opportunity of publicly sharing those views in print or in the media. There are only oblique references in Marxist writings to other than Marxist social opinions regarding the churches in their countries apart from the feelings of the believers.

The literature on the subject is very scant. This is even more the case with literature in the English language. While the Marxist attitude toward religion is gradually receiving more exposure in print and is increasing by receiving Marxist scholarly attention, these views are written mostly in the languages of the various Eastern European countries. Only very few booklets, usually of informative or propaganda nature were published in English by Eastern European authorities in order to be distributed to those Westerners inquiring about religious liberties and the position of the churches (092, 120, 255, 407, 408). Invariably these tend to be products of bureaucrats in charge of church affairs who try to point out constitutional and legal guarantees of the freedom of religion and separation of church and state and to provide meager information on the work of the churches. Few have explored the reasons why Communists have opted for antireligious policies apart from the oft repeated cliches that the Russian Orthodox Church had been a supporter of the Czarist regime and that Marx considered religion to be the opiate of the people, thus preventing progress.

Marxist theory stipulates the withering away of religion in a future communist society, with the process commencing already under socialism. But Marxists differ in their perceptions of how this is to be achieved. Some Marxists prefer the rationalistic propagation of the atheist views of the Enlightenment, believing that when believers are educated in scientific views about life they will voluntarily drop their religious convictions. Others believe that as socialism raises the economic well-being of the masses and removes misery and poverty, people will no longer need to resort to religion as a means to cope with misery and alienation. In the meantime, Marxists may need to make compromises with religious groups and institutions. Still others believe that religion must be combated by administrative measures (029, 030). Legislative obstacles and prohibitions, bureaucratic intrusions and arbitrariness, trials, imprisonment, and torture characterize this approach. The harshness of these measures vary from region to region and from one time period to another.

Recently there have been Marxist scholars, usually a minority, who believe that all three of these views are incompatible with a mature Marxist approach. They maintain that religion must be given full democratic legal protection by the socialist state just as the right to atheist propaganda is to be granted, but that the most fundamental liberation which the socialist state ought to promote is the liberation from all kinds of dependencies. When human beings, individually and socially, experience full self-determination, it is argued, the dependence upon a higher power will become unnecessary and people will gradually cease to be theists. In the meantime, the role of religion in society ought to be measured entirely by assessing whether religion is helpful to the workers' movement or is hindering it. If it is helpful, the Communist party ought to cooperate with religious people and institutions and if it is hindering then it ought to combat this particular religious group. This moves the focus from ideological to more pragmatic political grounds, even on a theoretical level. It ought to be pointed out that so far only the rationalist propagation view and this latter more comprehensive pragmatic Marxist approach have been defended in literature. Generally these views are practiced in life without written theoretical defense.

The Soviet Model

Religious policies of all Eastern European Communist parties were patterned after the religious policies of the Communist Party of the Soviet Union. Variations in religious policies, which do indeed exist, were forced upon the respective Communist parties by the greatly varied historical, national, and religious circumstances in their own lands to which the Party policies had to adjust. The Soviet example remained clear and undiluted.

The Soviet Bolsheviks have, from the outset, tended to differentiate their party's ideological stance toward religion from their constitutional approach. The Leninistic principle toward religion was that the party must combat religion as a vestige of the old bourgeoise system. Party members must embrace atheism and reject religious practices, but additionally it is their task to combat religion in any way possible. Hence "militant atheism" became not only an attitude but also was institutionalized in organizations of militant atheists (142).

Legally, religion was separated from the state and declared to be a private matter of each individual citizen. Constitutional guarantees were made about freedom of conscience and worship, while atheists alone were given the right to propagate their views. Legislation provides for stiff penalties for the abuse of religion and making hostile statements or threatening the interest of the state. These legal provisions are purposively vaguely phrased so as to give wide discretionary powers to administrative officials in their task of restricting religious behavior (025). Most of legal guarantees have little meaning because the judiciary is completely subjected to the executive branch of the government, while the entire government is monopolized by the Communist party. The government is the implementor of the policies of the Communist party. The state is viewed as the instrument of the working class, but the Communist party is regarded as the sole possessor of Marxist scientific knowledge of what is in the best interest of the working class, while the Central Committee, and more specifically the Politbureau and even more so the General Secretary of the party in fact determines the party's policies. Thus it is that policies toward religion are determined at the center, and modifications in tactics, though not in strategy, occur according to exigencies to which the ruling elite responds with greater or lesser rigidity (093). Regional variations within the Soviet Union occur as such policies have to be implemented with the sensitivities of national groups and traditions taken into account (059, 069). Thus there are inconsistencies in the tactical approach to religion, but the strategy remains consistently targeted to the elimination of religion as quickly as possible (053). Timetables for destruction have had to be revised and extended (076, 085). Some religious groups are perceived as more dangerous to the socialist project and are consequently more vehemently attacked (e.g., Ukrainian Uniates and unregistered Baptists) or more strictly controlled (Russian Orthodox Church) (105, 109, 110, 119, 124). Often the government's policy toward a religion reflects that religion's linkage with nationalism and the government's attempt to deal with nationality problems. Usually this is to the disadvantage of the churches except in a few cases such as the Romanian Orthodox Church.

Other Eastern European Countries

The only Communist party which exceeded the Soviet Party in it's zeal to destroy religion is the Albanian, where claims have been made that religion has been totally eradicated (221, 223, 224, 225). No functioning church is known to exist.

If one were to construct a scale where the criterion was to be the rigor by which antireligious policies were implemented, certainly Albania would be at the extreme end for its most vicious supression of church life. Next to it one would place the Soviet Union and Bulgaria. The Soviet approach has been described above; the Bulgarians have consistently been the most docile followers of the Soviet example. In both countries religious groups are constantly subject to pressure and control.

In Bulgaria the Communists decided drastically to intimidate all of the churches by organizing show trials against the small, but heretofore influential Protestant community, thereby destroying the top leadership of these churches (230, 231). The attack on the churches in the late 1940s and throughout the fifties was brutal (226). Although relaxation of such measures took place afterwards, the Bulgarian government still very strictly supervises religious activities.

The Romanian Communists are also noted for their heavy hand in internal matters, but due to foreign policy differences with the Soviet Union and internal needs to manipulate a multinational state, the Romanian Communists have given their churches, in particular the Romanian Orthodox Church, more space for action, which manifests itself in very lively theological creativity, good church attendance, publishing activity, extensive ecumenical contacts, etc. (370-372). From time to time the Romanian government comes down with a heavy hand upon the less cooperative denominations. The Eastern Rite Catholics have thus been forcibly incorporated into the Roman Orthodox Church from the outset, and the rapidly growing Baptists have been harassed by the authorities even at the time when the authority's attitude toward the Orthodox Church was benevolent (362-364, 376).

On the other side of the scale would be the other five socialist countries of Eastern Europe, namely East Germany, Poland, Czechoslovakia, Hungary, and Yugoslavia. Each of them has had periods when the Communist government definitely relaxed its strictures against the churches, though no common pattern is to be found among them except that the period immediately after the Communist take-over was the harshest and most repressive and that later modifications ensued. In Czechoslovakia during the "Prague Spring" of 1968 perhaps the most liberal and enlightened Marxist policy toward religion was practiced (241) only to be subsequently reversed to a very oppressive and restrictive policy under heavy Soviet pressure. In the 1970s and 1980s the Czechoslovak government reverted to the policies of the 1950s. The Roman Catholic Church, the church of the majority of Czechs and Slovaks, is more supressed than the Protestant churches as it has been less willing to make accommodations to the government (235, 239, 243, 246).

In East Germany the ruling Socialist Unity Party has changed its policies from sharp criticism of the churches to a working relationship with the churches under which the government avoids deliberate provocations and grants fairly good conditions for church work, though not without certain restrictions. The Marxists apparently have come to the conviction that they stand more to gain from a cooperative than an antagonistic approach (278).

This is also the current policy of the Hungarian Communists. Antagonism has been replaced with cooperation and tolerance, which has by and large replaced the confrontational stance of the pre-1956 period. The Communist party feels it has a good working relationship with the churches and it is currently basking in the success which general liberalization has brought to Hungary, both economically and politically (206, 303).

The story of the Polish Communists' inability to handle the Roman Catholic Church has been oft repeated. They have never been able to drive a wedge between the Catholic Church and the people of Poland; and in view of the grave social, political, and economic problems that have beset the Polish Communists it has become obvious to them that they must not fight the Roman Catholic Church but negotiate with it (323, 325, 326, 336). Atheism is not a requirement for membership in the Polish United Workers' Party. Even the martial law period of General Jaruzelski did not diminish the need of the Polish United Worker's Party to seek at least a modicum of cooperation from the Catholic Church.

The policy of the Yugoslav Communists toward the churches is not very enlightened per se; nor have they ever had to face up to the enormous ecclesiastical power as in Poland, though they privately admit to the strong influence of the churches. The change from persecution to tolerance came about due to the evolution of the entire Yugoslav socialist system moving away from Stalinism. One should look to the inner dynamics of the process of liberalization of Yugoslav socialism to find the clue to a more liberal attitude toward the church, which, however, varies regionally. Attempts at administrative supervision still exist, though little attempt is made to control or infiltrate the churches (400).

Factors Influencing Religious Policy

The informed observer who notices such diversity in religious policies of different communist parties and governments comes to an obvious conclusion that religious policies are not dictated or coordinated by Moscow. This is true not only of the Albanians and Yugoslavs who have departed from the block, or Romania, the uncooperative block member, but even for the others who normally consult Moscow. While inspiration on all ideological matters does come from Moscow, one need not resort to a conspiracy theory that such matters are decided in Moscow and implemented in the various other capitals. The similarities in religious policies can be adequately explained by their common Marxist-Leninist inspirations and by the general Soviet pressures for ideological conformity.The differences arise due to the practical problems encountered in attempting to implement Marxism-Leninism under most varied concrete situations.

In this implementation two Marxist protagonists play a role. The first are the Councils for Church Affairs (024). They go under various titles and ministries in different countries, but in each case they consist of bureaucracies set up by the communist government to deal with the churches. Sometimes there is also a department dealing with churches within the police or security forces. In these Councils Communist bureaucrats determine how to deal with churches on a day to day basis. They also recommend policies, legislation, and decrees to the higher government organs, or implement directives from above. In times of great conflict these councils are headed and staffed by people very antagonistic to churches whose aim is to break the back of the churches. On the other hand, when general liberalization has taken place, enlightened Marxists (or on occasion "progressive" priests who have learned to cooperate with the government) are appointed who show more flexibility and understanding and who attempt to be liaisons between church and state. On a few occasions the churches considered the heads of such councils as being friendly to the wellbeing of the churches (e.g., Dr. Erika Kadlecova in Czechoslovakia in 1968 or Zlatko Frid in Croatia at about the some time). However, more often than not, these councils are staffed either by nondescript bureaucrats of limited intellectual capacities or by people who believe their task to be to speed up the "withering away of religion."

The other quite different group consists of Marxist scholars of religion. In the earlier phases of the communist rule there was little scholarly interest in religion. However, subsequently, a limited number of scholars turned their attention to religion. One may discern two types of scholars: one in the service of their ideology (078), and the other, fewer in number, searching for truth in their academic discipline (411, 412).

The first group studies religion in order to find its weak points and to provide atheist propaganda as a tool to overcome religion. This dogmatic ideological approach is unscientific because its methodology consists of deductions from the postulates, assumptions, and sporadic observations or judgments of Marx and Lenin, neither of whom were particularly knowledgeable about religion or church life. Practically all the Soviet scholars, mostly sociologists of religion, perceive themselves to be in the service of atheist education (078). Rarely do they say anything positive about a church. One finds similar scholars in other socialist countries.

Their counterpart is a group of Marxist scholars who regard religion as an important human activity in the contemporary analysis of society. These humanistic Marxists scholars are actually the first Marxists to follow a scientific or scholarly investigation of religion, though some of them also suffer from an antireligious bias. They have sometimes questioned the assumptions of the classics of Marxism, and at other times tried to present a more balanced critique of religion in which they see not only the faults of churches but also their positive contributions (029, 037). These studies are not infused with hostility, nor are they intended deliberately to speed up the destruction of religion. Among such scholars are Janusz Kuczyński, Milan Machovec, Vitezsláv Gardavský, Jószef Lukács, Esad Ćimić, Zdenko Roter, Branko Bošnjak, Srdjan Vrcan, Andrija Krešić, and Marko Keršhevan. Sometimes this latter group comes into conflict with the bureaucrats of the Council on Church Affairs or with the party ideologists, but occasionally their interpretation prevails and becomes the stated policy of the Council on Church Affairs, as is the case of Jószef Lukács's views in Hungary (285, 303).

The empirical studies of these humanistic Marxist scholars of religion have brought unexpected answers as to the degree of religiosity of the population, especially among that sector which, from the Marxist ideological viewpoint, should be the least religious, namely the working class. These studies as well as the demands of the striking Polish workers and of "Solidarity," their labor union, show that in many instances the working class is quite attached to religion. They point out the greater impact of secularization upon religion, which is often less the result of atheist propaganda or class consciousness and more the result of urbanization, industrialization, higher education, and the general disintegration of traditional societal norms, including morality (341). Some of them do not see this process as altogether desirable from the Marxist viewpoint, noting that secularization is often accompanied by some very negative social abberations: e.g., alcoholism, apathy, loss of moral constraints, and escapism. It would appear that future researchers studying the impact of society on religion, Marxists and non-Marxists alike, would do well to consider the processes characteristic of many modern industrial societies, in which many traditional values, including religious ones, have been eroding or have disappeared altogether. The churches do not seem to have the stamina or the vision to come to grips with these new challenges. One gets the impression that the Communist parties are likewise unimaginative in facing up to these social processes to which they contributed but with which they do not know how to cope.

Finally, one should mention non-Marxist social forces in Eastern European societies which are not religiously oriented (049, 050). This is an amorphous group. The vast majority consist of people perhaps indifferent to churches. Some might be slightly critical of churches, others slightly sympathetic; but the general situation mandates a distance from churches and no ostensible signs of interest (though from time to time groups, especially of young people, get attracted to a given church because of imaginative religious services -- e.g., rock masses, peace concerns, beautiful liturgy and music, challenging preaching -- or social rebellion). In this strata of the population are also some nonMarxist intellectuals who, in their creative works (usually literature, but sometimes also film, theater, intellectual history, restoration of monuments, etc.), sometimes show a deep respect for spiritual values and sympathy to religious groups that foster those values (051).

Conclusion

If one is to evaluate the overall success of the Communist policies toward religion, one may say that they seem to have more failures than successes. The ultimate goal of the destruction of churches is not within sight, except in Albania. (From a strictly implementational viewpoint, one may judge the Albanian Communist Party as most successful in stamping out church life). Churches still play an important social role, and in some instances, such as in Poland, a decisive role. On the other hand, Communist policies have been successful in diminishing the influence of the churches on public life. No more are church and state so closely identified. On the whole churches have lost many of their former members and do not have a strong foothold among the young. Many institutional forms of religion have suffered great, perhaps permanent setbacks. Some churches have become the focus of dissent; they are one of the very few alternate viewpoints to the official ideology. Many churches have purified their style of operation and those that have not compromised their spiritual commitment have gained the respect of wide segments of the population for integrity and concerns for human values. Some churches were outwardly domesticized and rendered less dangerous to the system. Yet on the whole there is much reason for the concern that many Communists have about churches: they remain the protagonists of an alternate lifestyle and set of values, which, ultimately, may be more lasting than the Marxist vision.

The experiences of church life under socialism make it unlikely that the churches would want to return simply to the presocialist stage. Some of the positive values of socialism -- such as the desire for human dignity, equality, social services, and attempts to elevate the standards of the poor (which often remain more part of socialist aspiration than achievement) -- are well suited to be adopted as part of the Christian agenda. It is impossible to know which way Eastern European Christians would go in the future if they were completely free. But they have learned the lessons of socialism, some very bitter and some positive. It is likely that these experiences have become a permanent part of their historical heritage, which will shape their actions for years to come.

The basic question remains as to whether the socialist state is able to evolve away from an anticlericalist or atheist (i.e., *anti*-theist) position in which the state is fundamentally hostile to religion and to a true separation of church and state, where the state is simply *non*-theist without making atheism the new state religion. Many in Eastern Europe aspire to reach the level of development in which the government will cease to interfere in religious matters, neither promoting any particular religion or atheism nor prohibiting it. Then religion and atheism would be truly free. That is a precondition for true freedom.

Bibliographical Survey

AREA-WIDE

001. Anderson, Paul. "Religious Liberty Under Communism." *Journal of Church and State* 6 (1964): 169-177.

    An overview of the dilemmas of churches in Eastern Europe, with an emphasis on the USSR by one of the best American Protestant experts on church life under Communism. Though changes since 1964 have rendered a few of the revisions obsolete, the article is still an insightful and dependable interpretation.

002. Azrael, Jeremy R. "Communism, Religion and the Churches." *Problems of Communism* 11, no. 5 (September-October 1962).

    A book review article which includes Walter Kolarz's *Religion in the Soviet Union* (089) and Constantine de Grunwald's *The Churches and the Soviet Union* (082). Azrael is appreciative of the first and very critical of the second book. He holds that the relationship between communism and religion is inherently unstable.

003. Barron, J. B., and H. M. Waddams, eds. *Communism and the Churches: A Documentation.* New York: Morehouse-Gorham Company, 1950.

    A selection of pronouncements and statements of representative authorities about churches in Eastern Europe and USSR on church-state relations.

004. Bastenier, Albert, ed. "Religion and the Churches Function in Socialist Societies." *Social Compas* 28, no. 1 (1981): 1-119.

Articles on Hungary, Yugoslavia, Poland, G.D.R. and Romania in French and English mostly by Eastern European sociologists, Marxist and Christian. Emphasizes social change and the church and church-state relations.

005. Beeson, Trevor. *Discretion and Valour: Religious Conditions in Russia and Eastern Europe.* Glasgow: Collins (Fontana Books), 1974, Rev. ed., Philadelphia: Fortress Press, 1982.

A country by country comprehensive account of the religious situation in socialist countries from the Communist take-over to the present. It includes evolution of church-state, theological, ecumenical, and socio-ethical issues. Wealth of data and sound interpretation. Represents the work of a study commission of the British Council of Churches. A fundamentally important book and a most reliable scholarly guide to the position of churches in Eastern European societies. Indispensable to libraries and individual readers. Useful to both expert and general reader.

006. Bennett, John C. *Christianity and Communism Today.* New York: Association Press, 1962.

A scholarly exploration of the nature of Communism and a suggested American Christian response. Helpful in understanding Communist goals from the perspective of a liberal Protestant theologian. Marginal references on religion and society in socialist countries.

007. Blanchard, Paul. *Communism, Democracy and Catholic Power.* Boston: The Beacon Press, 1951.

The author pictures a three-way struggle between democracy and totalitarianism of the Kremlin and the Vatican. The author is both anti-Communist and anti-Catholic. Only occasionally are there glimpses of religious issues in the USSR and Eastern Europe.

008. *The Church Under Communism.* New York: Philosophical Library, 1953.

009. Cockburn, J. Hutchison. *Religious Freedom in Eastern Europe.* Richmond, VA: John Knox Press, 1953.

A narrative of the suppression of religious liberties (as defined at the outset of the book) in Russia, East Germany, Poland, Czechoslovakia, Hungary, Yugoslavia, Romania, and Bulgaria. Written at a time when only the most brutal suppressions were in evidence. Needs to be tempered by evidence from later, less severely oppressive periods.

010. D'Arcy, Martin C. *Communism and Christianity.* New York: The Devin-Adair Company, 1957.

A comparison between Communism and Christianity on the level of ideas. Relatively little material devoted to post World War II encounter in Eastern Europe and that tends to be scattered throughout the book.

011. Daim, Wilfred. *The Vatican and Eastern Europe*. Trans. by Alexander Gode. New York: Frederick Ungar Publishing Co., 1970.

A critical interpretation of the role of the Vatican and the Roman Catholic Church in the USSR and Eastern Europe, particularly Poland. Frequent references to the interaction of church in society both historically and in the present.

012. Dunn, Dennis J., ed. *Religion and Communist Society*. Berkley: Berkley Slavic Specialties, 1983.

Six scholarly papers presented at the Second World Congress for Soviet and East European Studies in Garmisch-Partenkirchen, West Germany, in 1980. Four deal with the USSR, and one each with Bulgaria and Romania. The editor considers the essays to be a testimony to a revival of religion in Eastern Europe since the 1970s.

013. *The Encounter of the Church with Movements of Social Change in Various Cultural Contexts*. Geneva, Switzerland: Department of Studies, Lutheran World Federation, 1977.

Papers from two symposia on Lutheran responses to various movements of social change, especially to Marxism. Papers on East Germany (Hanspeter Wulff - Woesten, Heino Falcke and Gottfried Bierman) and Hungary (Béla Harmáti) as well as committee analyses which take into account a theological response to Marxism in those two countries. Very sound theological reflections and dependable insights on the church's response to society.

014. Galter, Albert. *The Red Book of the Persecuted Church*. Westminster, MD: Newman Press, 1957.

Exclusive focus on the persecution of the Roman Catholic Church in each of the Eastern European countries and the Soviet Union until the early 1950s makes this a book of limited use today. Only the failures of the Communist governments are noted. Heavily biased in favor of the Catholic Church.

015. de George, Richard T., and Scanlan, James P. *Marxism and Religion in Eastern Europe*. Dordrecht and Boston: D. Reidel Publishing Co., 1974.

Second part of the book (pp. 93-175) is devoted to Eastern Europe, though only three articles deal with post-World War II: one on the oppression of the Ukrainian Uniates (by Vasyl Markus), one on the dissenters in the USSR (by Bohdan Bociurkiw), and the last on Muslim religious dissent in the USSR (by Alexandre Benningsen and S. Enders Wimbush). Scholarly analyses.

016. Greinacher, Norbert, and Virgil Elizando, eds. *Churches in Socialist Societies in Eastern Europe.* New York: Seabury Press, 1982.

A Concilium issue by diverse authors, both Eastern European and Western, on various aspects of church life. Among the authors are East German, Lutheran Bishop Albrecht Schönherr, Yugoslav Catholic Auxiliary Bishop Vekoslav Grmič, Hungarian sociologist Emmerich András, and Polish Catholic Władysław Piwowarski.

017. Grossu, Sergiu. *The Church in Today's Catacombs.* Translated by Janet L. Johnson. New Rochelle, NY: Arlington House Publishers, 1975.

A series of unrelated short fragments, many dealing with persecution of Christians in Eastern Europe. No attempt at analysis but a self-proclaimed "book of accusations" on behalf of the "Church of Silence." Not a dependable source.

018. Gsovski, Vladimir, ed. *Church and State Behind the Iron Curtain.* New York: Frederick A. Praeger, 1955.

Articles by teams of scholars on Czechoslovakia, Hungary, Poland, and Romania with an introductory chapter on separation of church and state in the USSR by Gsovski. Prepared by the Mid-European Law Project, the book helpfully focuses on legal cases against the churches and provides extensive translations of laws regulating religious life. (*See also* 226, 240, 288, 393)

019. Hebly, J. A. "Churches in Eastern Europe: Three Models of Church-State Relations and Their Relevance for the Ecumenical Movement." *Occasional Papers on Religion in Eastern Europe* 4, no. 3 (May 1984). 14-37.

Comparison of three different models of church-state relations, namely the Russian Orthodox Church with the Soviet state, the Hungarian Protestant Church with the Hungarian state and the East German Protestant churches with their government.

020. Hutten, Kurt. *Iron Curtain Christians: The Church in Communist Countries Today.* Translated by Walter G. Tillmanns. Minneapolis: Augsburg Publishing House, 1967.

A comprehensive survey of post-war developments in each of the Eastern European countries (and China) to the early 1960s. Registers primarily the persecuting aspects of church-state relations. Provides many legal texts and many authoritative pronouncements.

021. King, Robert R., and James F. Brown, eds. *Eastern Europe's Uncertain Future*. New York: Praeger Publishers, 1977.

Two Radio Free Europe research reports on the religious situation in Poland and Hungary. Thomas E. Henegham's "The Loyal Opposition: Party Programs and Church Response in Poland," (pp. 286-300) and Charles E. Kovats' "The Path of Church-State Reconciliation in Hungary," (pp. 301-311). Analysis of developments in the 1970s. (See 326 and 299 respectively.)

022. DeKoster, Lester. **Communism and Christian Faith.** Grand Rapids: Wm. B. Eerdmans Publishing Company, 1962.

023. Kuzmič, Peter. "Evangelical Witness in Eastern Europe." In **Serving Our Generation: Evangelical Strategies for the Eighties.** Edited by Waldron Scott. (Colorado Springs: WEF, 1980): 77-85.

 A brief overview of the status and problems of evangelical churches in the USSR and Eastern Europe with an evaluation of their tasks and problems.

024. Luchterhandt, Otto. "State Authorities for Religious Affairs in Soviet Bloc Countries." **Religion in Communist Lands** 13, no. 1 (Spring 1985): 54-62.

 A study of the state regulatory agencies for religious affairs shows how varied is the situation of churches in various socialist societies, despite the common basic hostility of these states to religion. (*See also* 114)

025. Luchterhandt, Otto. "The Understanding of Religious Freedom in the Socialist States." **Occasional Papers on Religion in Eastern Europe** 3, no.3 (April 1983): 15-26.

 After examining the special place of religious liberty in jurisprudence and in the writings of Marx and Lenin, the author examines the discrepancies in the degree of religious freedom in Eastern Europe, contrasting particularly the Soviet Union and East Germany.

026. MacEoin, Gary. **The Communist War on Religion.** New York: Devin-Adair Co., 1951.

027. Markham, R. H. **Communists Crush Churches in Eastern Europe.** Boston: Meader Publishing Co., 1951.

028. Mitrokhin, Lev N. "On 'Dialogue' Between Marxists and Christians." **Soviet Studies in Philosophy** 10, no. 4 (Spring 1972): 337-361.

 Translation of article from **Voprosy Filozofii** (Moscow) in which author blames dialogue for subversion of Marxist positions. Presents the Soviet Marxist view.

029. Mojzes, Paul. **Christian-Marxist Dialogue in Eastern Europe.** Minneapolis, MN: Augsburg Publishing House, 1981.

 A comprehensive account of Christian-Marxist dialogues in all socialist countries of Eastern Europe (including USSR and Yugoslavia), providing a history, analysis and typology of dialogues. Shows interaction of Christian thought with Marxism. Scholarly study.

030. Mojzes, Paul. "Christian-Marxist Dialogue in Eastern Europe: 1945-1980." <u>Occasional Papers on Religion in Eastern Europe</u> 4, no. 4 (July 1984): 13-53.

Area-wide and country-by-country survey of the history of Christian-Marxist dialogue, with a typology of these encounters. Author views dialogue as the best alternative type of encounter.

031. Mojzes, Paul. "Impact of the Eastern European Churches Upon Their Own Societies." <u>Occasional Papers on Religion in Eastern Europe</u> 2, no. 7 (November 1982): 1-25.

The variety and source of social influences of churches classified into models. The church's attitude toward socialism and areas of greatest impact are examined.

032. Mojzes, Paul, ed. <u>Varieties of Christian-Marxist Dialogue.</u> Philadelphia: The Ecumenical Press, 1978.

Along with a survey of the status of the Christian - Marxist dialogue which contains references to Eastern Europe, the symposium contains contributions by Andrija Krešić and Jakov Romić (Yugoslavia), József Lukács (Hungary) and Adolf Niggemeier (East Germany). Shows Christian - Marxist dialogue in Yugoslavia, Hungary, and East Germany at different stages, with different emphases. The value of the volume is found in the exposure of various attitudes toward dialogue.

033. Peachey, Paul. "Religion in Soviet Marxist Societies: Ideology and <u>Realpolitik</u>." <u>Occasional Papers on Religion in Eastern Europe</u> 4, no. 3 (May 1984): 1-13.

Examines shifting relationships between churches and society, noting ambiguities under Soviet-type socialism. The main source of the official hostility to religion stems from the Communist monistic conception of reality.

034. Ramet, Pedro, ed. <u>Religion and Nationalism in Soviet and East European Politics.</u> Durham, NC: Duke University Press, 1984.

Explorations of the exceptionally close link between nationalism and religion in the USSR (specifically Russia, Ukraine, and Lithuania), Poland, Hungary, Yugoslavia, Romania, and Bulgaria, with a few comparative analyses. Among contributors are Ramet, Scarf, Pospielovsky, Markus, Laszlo, and Chrypinski. A scholarly symposium of high quality. (<u>See also</u> 170)

035. "Religion and Churches Function in Socialist Societies." <u>Social Compass</u> 28, no. 1 (1981): 1-119.

Articles dealing with religion and secularism in socialist societies mostly by sociologists such as Srdjan Vrcan, Miklós Tomka, Jakov Jukić, J. Marianki, and A. King. A few other articles are in French.

036. Romanyuk, Vasyl. *A Voice in the Wilderness.* Wheaton, IL: Society for the Study of Religion under Communism, 1980.

037. Roter, Zdenko. "A Marxist View of Christianity." *Journal of Ecumenical Studies* 9, no. 1 (Winter 1972): 40-50.

The views of the Yugoslav humanistic Marxist sociologist from Slovenia stressing positive elements in Christianity and advocating dialogue. Reconciling posture.

038. Runciman, Steven. *The Orthodox Churches and the Secular State.* Auckland: Auckland University Press and Oxford University Press, 1971.

Last part of the book presents patterns of Orthodox church-state relations in Russia and the Balkans with a wealth of historical material on preceeding periods. Concise explanation of Orthodox ability to survive hostile regimes. Scholarly lectures.

039. Sawatsky, Walter. "Power in Church-State Relations in Eastern Europe." *Mennonite Quarterly Review* 55 (July 1981): 214-217.

040. Shuster, George N. *Religion Behind the Iron Curtain.* New York: The Macmillan Co., 1954.

An account of the Communist attack upon religion written at the height of the Cold War attempting to draw to attention the suffering of the churches and the brutality of the oppressors.

041. Solyom-Fekete, William. *The Church and State under Communism: A Special Study.* Washington: U.S. Government Printing Office, 1965: 1-11.

Status of churches and laws regulating religion.

042. Stehle, Hansjakob. *Eastern Politics of the Vatican, 1917-1979.* Athens, OH: Ohio University Press, 1981.

Primary interest of the author is to trace the changing *Ostpolitik* of the Vatican but marginally the church-society interactions are noted by this important German obsrever of the Vatican.

043. Tobias, Robert. *Communist-Christian Encounter in East Europe.* Indianapolis, IN: School of Religion Press, 1956.

A study of the subjugation of churches in the USSR, Rumania, Bulgaria, Albania, Poland, Hungary, Czechoslovakia, and East Germany both on a regional level and with a detailed country-by-country chronology of events to 1951. Includes rich documentation and texts of legislation. A comprehensive, scholarly, balanced presentation written toward the end of the Stalinist era. A dependable guide; one of the best books emerging out of the Stalinist period, still in many ways unsurpassed.

044. Udy, James S. *Christians and Churches in Socialist Countries.* Delhi, India: ISPCK, 1982.

Report of a visit by church leaders from Southeast Asia and Australia to the Christian Peace Conference, East Germany, Czechoslovakia, and USSR. A superficial narration of impressions from an officially sponsored trip. Gives insight into official church leaders' views.

045. Weingärtner, Erich, ed. *Church Within Socialism.* Rome: IDOC International, 1976.

Based on the work of Giovanni Barberini, this book contains studies, reports, legislation, and other documentation, often previously published. Covers all socialist states of Eastern Europe both regionally and individually. Often excerpts from a variety of publications are presented without enough interpretative comment. Provides both religious and Marxist views. A book welcomed by some church people in Eastern Europe as reliable; however, at times analysis is lacking or shallow. An important book, nevertheless, which needs to be consulted by all who are doing investigation in the field because it contains rare source material. (*See also* 303)

046. Walters, Philip. "Christians in Eastern Europe: a Decade of Aspirations and Frustrations." *Religion in Communist Lands* 11, no. 1 (Spring 1983): 6-24.

Without specifying the decade -- the author actually surveys events of the 1960s, 1970s, and into the 1980s -- the author asseses the achievements and setbacks of religious groups, primarily Christian, in all Eastern European countries. A good short overview.

047. Wild, Georg. *Protestantism in Eastern Middle Europe.* Translated by Franz Schultz. Leer, Ostfriesl: Gerhard Rantenberg, 1963.

Concise historical survey of Protestantism from the Reformation until today with short factual statements about the post-World War II period.

048. Yule, Robert M., ed. *Religion in Communist Countries: A Bibliography of Books in English.* Wellington: New Zealand Society for the Study of Religion and Communism, 1979. (*See also* 075).

Lists major books and individual contributions to symposia in the USSR, Eastern Europe, China, and Southeast Asia with brief comments.

049. Zademach, Wieland. "The 'Fifth International?': Dissidents in Eastern Europe." *LWF Marxism and China Study Information Letter* 30 (August,1980): 1-14.

Survey of dissident movements in Eastern Europe including religious dissenters in the USSR, Poland and Czechoslovakia.

050. Zademach, Wieland. "The 'Fifth International?': Dissidents in Eastern Europe." Occasional Papers on Religion in Eastern Europe 1, no. 6 (November 1981):10-20.

Describes the different kinds of dissidents in the Soviet Union (e.g. Neo-Marxists, Ethical Socialists, Liberals, Neo-Slavophiles and Democratic Nationalists), the Committee for Social Self-Defense in Poland, and Charter 77 in Czechoslovakia.

INDIVIDUAL COUNTRIES

UNION OF SOVIET SOCIALIST REPUBLICS

General

051. Agursky, Mikhail. "The Attitude to Religion in the New Russian Literature." Religion in Communist Lands 10, no. 2 (Fall 1982): 145-154.

An oblique introduction to religious themes in Russian national literature. Among the themes are religion as pragmatic value, search for God, pantheistic ideas and defense of Russian Orthodoxy.

052. Anderson, Paul B. People, Church and State in Modern Russia. London: Student Christian Movement Press, 1944.

The author is mostly dealing with pre-war and war developments, but notes that some area of cooperation between the West and Russia is possible due to common endeavor during WW II.

053. Andreev, I. A. "Soviet Local Authorities Combat Religion (Moldavia SSR)." Religion in Communist Lands 7 (Autumn 1979): 184-190.

Details how local authorities in Moldavia combat religion and the variety of organizations involved in anti-religious work.

054. Bach, Marcus. God and the Soviets. New York: Thomas Y. Crowell Company, 1958.

Impressions of the status of churches in the USSR based on a one month trip in 1957 blending it with research. Popularly written narrative, with many recorded conversations and experiences.

055. Baker, Alonzo L. Religion in Russia Today. Nashville: Southern Publishing Association, 1967.

An introductory survey of religious groups and their contemporary situation. A clearly written short explanation of the status of religion in the USSR.

056. Beeson, Trevor. "Russia Tightens the Squeeze on Religious Dissidents." Christian Century 97 (May 7, 1980): 510-512.

057. Bociurkiw, Bohdan R., "Church-State Relations in the USSR" Survey (January 1968):4-32.

058. Bociurkiw, Bohdan R., "Religion in the USSR after Khrushchev." The Soviet Union under Brezhnev and Kosygin, edited by John W. Strong, 135-155. New York: Van Nostrand, 1971.

059. Bociurkiw, Bohdan R., "The Shaping of Soviet Religious Policy." Problems of Communism 22, no. 3 (May-June 1973).

Soviet policies toward religion are more inconsistent than claimed either by the Soviets or Western sources. The author charts some of the reversals of policy and the rise of new religious and non-religious interest groups which will necessitate a reassessment of policies by the authorities due to the changes going on in Soviet society.

060. Boiter, Albert. Religion in the Soviet Union. Washington: Sage Publishers, 1980.

061. Bolshakoff, Serge. Russian Nonconformity: The Story of "Unofficial" Religion in Russia. Philadelphia: The Westminster Press, 1950.

A historical survey of non-conformist religion in Russia of which only shorter segments toward the end of the book deal with the post-WW II period. Helpful for understanding of minority non-conforming religious traditions.

062. Bourdeaux, Michael and Michael Rowe, eds. May One Believe - in Russia?: Violations of Religious Liberty in the Soviet Union. London: Darton, Longman and Todd, 1980.

An introduction to religion in Russia and a documented account of ways in which religion is being repressed in the USSR.

063. Bourdeaux, Michael. Opium of the People: The Christian Religion in the USSR. London: Faber and Faber, 1965.

Observations, analyses, and critiques based on Bourdeax's studies and residence in the USSR in 1959/60, highlighting both the vitality and restrictions characterizing Soviet Christianity. He encountered many obstacles in making even routine contacts with clergy. The book is marked by concern for a Russian Christianity untainted by Communism and criticism of various forms of collaboration. A good basic survey of the history and current position of churches in society.

064. Bordeaux, Michael, Hans Hebly, and Eugen Voss, eds. *Religious Liberty in the Soviet Union: WCC and USSR - A Post-Nairobi Documentation.* Kent: Keston College and others, 1976.

A study of Soviet legislation on religion and a description of the struggle for religious liberty among all churches in the Soviet Union. (*See also* 139)

065. Bourdeaux, Michael. *Risen Indeed: Lessons in Faith from the USSR.* London: Darton, Longman and Todd, 1983.

A picture of religious experiences of Soviet Christians, their suffering and their faith.

066. Bourdeaux, Michael. "The Russian Church, Religious Liberty and the World Council of Churches." *Religion in Communist Lands* 13, no. 1 (Spring 1985): 4-27.

While the focus of the article is a critique of the World Council of Churches' policies, one can also gain a good deal of insight about the lack of religious liberty in the USSR.

067. Braun, Leopold L. S., *Religion in Russia.* Patterson, NJ: St. Anthony Guild Press, 1959.

The author, a Roman Catholic priest and former chaplain to the U.S. embassy in Moscow, described the state of religion from Lenin to Khrushchev. Only the last 10-15 pages deal with the situation after World War II. Maintains that no change whatsoever took place in the government's attitude to religion except some temporary expediencies.

068. Ciszek, Walter J., S.J., *With God in Russia.* New York: McGraw-Hill, 1964.

Autobiographical narrative of an American Jesuit captured by Russians in Poland in 1939 who lived several decades, mostly in Soviet prison camps, in the Urals and Siberia. A thoughtful description of conditions, including religious observances among Soviet prisoners. A fascinating account with no sensationalism. (*See also* 084, 103)

069. Conguest, Robert, ed. *Religion in the USSR.* New York: Frederick A. Praeger, Publishers, 1968.

Development of the state's policies toward religion examined in stages. Emphasis is on the state's oppressive policies toward religion based primarily on reports from Soviet newspapers. Provides a view of the state's anti-religious measures from their own journalistic reports.

070. Dunn, Dennis J., ed. *Religion and Modernization in the Soviet Union.* Boulder: Westview Press, 1977.

A series of eleven scholarly papers, five generally dealing with religion and modernization and six as it relates to specific religious groups. Though disagreeing on the merits of modernization all authors agree that it has made an impact on religion, but it is debatable whether the state's impact or modernization itself has a greater influence. They point out that government interference in religious life impedes religious attempts to modernize, yet religion remains influential among masses. Included are papers by W. Fletcher. (See also 078, 079, 085, 097).

071. Dunn, Dennis J. "Religion and Nationalism in the USSR and China." Problems of Communism 29, no. 2 (March-April (1980): 64-67.

Book review essay dealing with V. Stanley Vardys' and Christel Lane's books. (See also 093, 192).

072. Dunn, Dennis J., "Religious Renaissance in the Soviet Union." Journal of Church and State. (Winter 1977): 21-36.

073. Dunn, Ethel, "The Importance of Religion in the Soviet Rural Community." In The Soviet Rural Community, edited by James R. Millar, 346-375. Urbana: University of Illinois Press, 1971.

074. Feinstein, Stephen C. "Politics and Religion in Russia." In Religion in the Making of Western Man, edited by F. Coppa (1974): 129-146.

075. Fletcher, William C., comp. Christianity in the Soviet Union: An Annotated Bibliography and List of Articles, Works in English. Los Angeles: Research Institute on Communist Strategy and Propaganda, University of Southern California, 1963. (See also 048).

Bibliography containing 588 entries, including translated articles from the Soviet press.

076. Fletcher, William C. "Reductive Containment: Soviet Religious Policy." Journal of Church Studies 2 (Fall 1980): 487-504.

077. Fletcher, William C. Religion and Soviet Foreign Policy 1945-1970. London: Royal Institute of International Affairs (O.V.P.), 1973.

A study of the advantages to Soviet foreign policy of the international activities of churches from the USSR and Eastern Europe. The foreign travel, bi-lateral agreement, the Christian Peace Conference, the World Council of Churches, and other activities are examined. The author concludes that churches are to various degrees used for goals of Soviet foreign policy. Some of Fletcher's deductions are forced and unbalanced.

078. Fletcher, William C. Soviet Believers: The Religious Sector of the Population. Lawrence: The Regents Press of Kansas, 1981.

A study of the number, age, gender, education, occupation, living conditions, social alienation, religious education, conversion, and world view of believers in the USSR based on the sociological data and studies of Soviet sociologists. Fletcher analyzes the strengths and weaknesses of Soviet sociological studies and reveals with some surprising and useful data on religious life in the Soviet Union in the context of a secular society. (See also 070, 079, 085, 097, 124, 204).

079. Fletcher, William C., and Anthony J. Strover, eds. Religion and the Search for New Ideals in the USSR. New York: Frederick A. Praeger, 1967.

Twelve scholarly papers from an international symposium at the Institute for the Study of the USSR in Munich held in 1966. They deal with issues ranging from alienation to Orthodoxy's relationship with youth, pseudo-religious Communist Party rituals, Jews and Muslims and religious themes in Soviet literature. (See also 070, 078, 085, 097).

080. Glazov, V., "Religious Values and Russian Political Dissent." Humanitas 15 (November 1979): 305-325.

081. Gossman, Joan Delaney. "Leadership of Antireligious Propaganda in the Soviet Union." Studies in Soviet Thought 12, no. 3 (September 1972).

082. de Grunwald, Constantine. The Churches in the Soviet Union. New York: MacMillan, 1962.

This translation from French of a book by a Russian immigrant who visited the USSR in 1960 focuses on the Orthodox Church with some attention to Old Believers and "Sectarians". Includes the issue of antireligious propaganda and chances for survival by the churches. Overly optimistic about the current government policies.

083. de Grunwald, Constantine. God and the Soviets. Trans. by G.J. Robinson-Paskevsky. London: Hutchinson, 1961.

A generally appreciative appraisal of the status of religion in the USSR by a Russian immigrant from France based on extensive experiences in the Soviet Union in the 1960. The methodology is recounting conversations and reviewing literature laced with historical references and personal evaluations of the author. The author's conclusion is that despite atheist advances religion still thrives in the USSR.

084. Hartfeld, Hermann. Faith Despite the KGB. Chappaqua, New York: Christian Herald Books, 1980.

Semi-fictional account of the experiences of a former Soviet prisoner held for his religious activities. (See also 068, 103, 200).

085. Hayward, Max, and Fletcher, William C. Religion and the Soviet State: A Dilemma of Power. New York: Frederick A. Praeger, Publishers, 1969.

Bringing together some of the most outstanding researchers in the field from Western Europe and North America this is a collection of eleven papers from a symposium at the Centre de Recherches et d'Etude des Institutions Religieuses in 1967 at Geneva. Includes a chapter on the Jewish question, on religion and nationalism, Soviet Islam, church-state questions, and others. High quality scholarly papers. (See also 070, 078, 079, 097).

086. Inkeles, Alex. Social Change in Soviet Russia. Cambridge: Harvard University Press, 1968.

Pp. 213-230 deal with the post-war position of the family and the church. Traces changes in church-state relations as evidences of social readjustments taking place in Soviet society.

087. Ivanov, Boris I., ed. Religion in the USSR. Research and Materials, Series I, no. 59. Translated by James Larkin. Munich: Institute for the Study of the USSR, 1960.

Anti-Communist emrigrees' accounts of the position of churches especially in the late 1950s, including accounts of the antireligious movement in the USSR.

088. Kline, George. Religious and Anti-religious Thought in Russia. Chicago: University of Chicago Press, 1968.

Pp. 152-171 provide a brief survey of the main post World War II issues in the USSR.

089. Kolarz, Walter. Religion in the Soviet Union. New York: St. Martin's Press, 1962.

This is a most comprehensive, balanced and authoritative account despite the author's bias against the Soviet government. The approach is denominational, surveying each religious group separately. Provides detailed study of all churches and their ability to survive within an atheistic society. Emphasis is on contemporary affairs, though a historical sketch of each group is also included.

090. Konstantinov, Dimitri. Religious Persecution in USSR. London, Canada: SBONB, 1965.

091. Kowalewski, David. "Religious Belief in the Brezhnev Era: Renaissance, Resistance and Realpolitik." Journal for the Scientific Study of Religion 19 (Spring 1980): 280-292.

092. Kuroyedov, Vladimir. Church and Religion in the USSR Moscow: Novosti Press Agency Publishing House, 1977.

Describes the status of religious bodies in the USSR in glowing terms maintaining that the Soviet government fully guarantees religious freedom. A propaganda tract by the highest government official in charge of religious affairs. Unreliable as a source.

093. Lane, Christel. Christian Religion in the Soviet Union: A Sociological Study. London: George Allen and Unwin, 1978; Albany, New York: State University of New York Press, 1978.

A comprehensive sociological analysis of nearly all major Soviet religious groups attempting to apply and test adequacy of Western sociological models. Study of social-demographic factors, causes for persistence or dissappearance of certain religious practices. Uses available sociological data from the Soviet Union. Monumental study of great scholarly importance. (See also 071).

094. Lane, C.O. "Some Explanations for the Persistence of the Christian Religion in the Soviet Union." Sociology 2 (1974).

095. Levitin-Krasnov, Anatoli. "Religion and Soviet Youth." Religion in Communist Lands 7, No. 4 (Winter 1979): 232-237.

Ideological vacuum caused by disillusionment with Marxism-Leninism is being filled for some youth by turning to religion. In cities they are mostly turning to Orthodoxy, especially the intelligentsia; in the country, to the sects. Thus religion comes to be an alternative for searching, dissatisfied and sensitive youth to whom society offers only vulgarities.

096. Lawrence, John. "Observations on Religion and Atheism in Soviet Society." Religion in Communist Lands 4, no. 5, 20-27.

097. Marshall, Richard H., ed. Aspects of Religion in the Soviet Union, 1917-1967. Chicago: University of Chicago Press, 1971.

A selection of twenty papers presented at two symposia to rectify lack of scholarly attention to religion in the Soviet Union. Five papers deal with the topic of religion and Soviet society (pp. 41-188), while twelve deal with specific religious groups in the USSR. One of the best scholarly symposia. Includes articles on the Armenian Apostolic Church by Mesrob Krikorian (164) and on the Georgian Orthodox Church by Elie Meha (165). (See also 070, 078, 079, 085).

098. Medlin, William K. "Social Change and Church Change." In Religious World of Russian Culture. 2nd ed. by Andrew Blane, (1975): 173-188.

099. Meerson-Aksenov, Michael and Boris Shragin, eds. *The Political, Social and Religious Thought of Russian Samizdat: An Anthology*. Translated by Nickolas Lapinin. Belmont, MA: Nordland Publishing Co., 1977.

A voluminous collection of the writings of the best known Soviet dissenters with Meerson-Aksenov's interpretive essays regarding the various *samizdat* topics. Part VIII (pp. 505-581) is entitled "The Problem of the Church in *Samizdat*" and contains, in addition to Meerson-Aksenov's writings, translations of A. Kolesov, E. Barabanov, and G. Iakunin and L. Regelson's appeals. These are responses to Alexander Solzhenitsyn's "Lenten Letter" to Patriarch Pimen (157) which provoked a lively discussion among the believing intelligentsia. (*See also* 113).

100. Melish, William Howard. *Religion Today in the Soviet Union*. New York: National Council of American-Soviet Friendship, 1945.

101. Murvar, Vatro. "Russian Religious Structures: A Study in Persistent Church Subservience." In *Journal for the Scientific Study of Religion* 7. no. 1 (1968): 1-22.

102. Newton, Louie. *An American Churchman in the Soviet Union.* New York: American Russian Institute, 1946.

103. Noble, John, and Glenn D. Everett. *I Found God in Soviet Russia*. New York: St. Martin's Press, 1959.

An account of the suffering of John Noble, an American Seventh-Day Adventist who was in Soviet prisons and camps in East Germany and the Soviet Union from 1945 to 1958. Provides evidence of interned clergy and believers as well as of spiritual revivals in Soviet prison camps. (*See also* 068, 084).

104. Paassen, Pierre Van. *Visions Rise and Change.* New York: The Dial Press, 1955.

A popularly written narrative of experiences of the author's frequent travels to the USSR, with many conversations with both officials and ordinary citizens. Most of the book deals with the pre-WW II period, with part III dealing with the post-Stalin era.

105. Pankhurst, Jerry. *The Orthodox and the Baptists in the USSR: Resources for the Survival of Ideologically Defined Deviance.* Ann Arbor: University Microfilms International, 1978.

106. Pankhurst, Jerry G. "Religion and Atheism in the USSR" In *Contemporary Soviet Society: Sociological Perspectives*. Edited by Jerry G. Pankhurst and Michael P. Sacks. 182-207. New York: Frederick A. Praeger, Publishers, 1980.

A sociological study of the impact of atheism and religion on Soviet society. The author argues that a mild resurgence of religiosity, particularly of a sectarian type, is taking place, which presents the government with a dilemma as to how to control them without causing further dissent.

107. Pankhurst, Jerry G. "The Strengths of Weak Parties in the Church-State Confrontations: The Soviet Religious Situation." In *Journal of Church and State* 26, no. 2 (Spring 1984): 273-291.

   Resources available to Russian Orthodox and Baptists in mobilizing their confrontation with the oppressive powerful atheist state. This is analyzed in terms of resources of power, context, history, ideology, and structure upon which each group can rely. There are also some less permanent resources such as the impact of World War II and pressure by concerned foreign persons or groups.

108. Parson, Howard L. *Christianity in the Soviet Union.* New York: American Institute for Marxist Studies, 1972.

   Follows predominantly an interview approach with both Communist and Christian spokespersons in the USSR. Deals with mutual relations. Reworded by a philosopher sympathetic to the Soviet Union but also positively inclined toward religion.

109. Powell, David E. *Antireligious Propaganda in the Soviet Union: A Study of Mass Persuasion.* Cambridge, MA: The M.I.T. Press, 1975.

   A detailed scholarly examination of various forms of antireligious propaganda, the organizations which promote it, and its effect upon the churches based on Soviet publication and Soviet and western sociological research. Based on very comprehensive investigation of primary sources. (*See also* 124, 142).

110. Ramet, Pedro. "Hypotheses on the Nationalities Factor in Soviet Religious Policy." *Occasional Papers on Religion in Eastern Europe* 2 (April 1985): 34-51.

   A series of hypotheses concerning the interrelationship of ethnicity and religion as it is reflected in Soviet government policies.

111. "Religion in the USSR." *Survey* 66 (January 1968): 4-125.

   Special emphasis issue with articles on church-state relations (Bohdan Bociurkiw), Soviet Baptists (Michael Bourdeaux and Peter Reddaway), religious themes in literature (Albert A. Todd), sects and survival of religion (Ethel Dunn) and others.

112. "Religious Problems in Russia Today." *Pro Mundi Vita* 58 (January 1976): 2-32. (*See also* 152).

113. Scarfe, Alan, ed. The CCDBR Documents: Christian Committee for the Defense of Believers' Rights in the USSR. Translated by Maria Belaetta.Glendale, CA: Door of Hope Press; and Orange, CA: Society for the Study of Religion under Communism, 1983.

Contains some of the most important documents on the position of religious people in the Soviet Union produced by dissenters who are critical both of the government and church authorities. Many documents poorly written and translated. (See also 099).

114. Roer, Ingo. "New Tendencies in State Policy Toward the Religious Groups in European Socialist Countries." Occasional Papers on Religion in Eastern Europe 4, no. 4 (July 1984): 1-12.

This article deals only with new elements in church-state relations in the USSR. Maintains that despite continuing difficulties many improvements have taken place. (See also 024).

115. Roshchin, Boris. "Soviet Weekly Attacks Four Churchmen." Religion in Communist Lands 5 (Autumn 1977): 186-191.

116. Rothenberg, Joshua. "The Status of Cults." Problems of Communism (Sept.-Oct. 1967): 119-124.

Provides decisions and legal acts of Soviet government regarding religion.

117. Sawatsky, Walter. "The New Soviet Law on Religion." Religion in Communist Lands 4 (Summer 1976): 4-10.

Soviet law of 1929 is often contradicted in practice. The legal revisions of 1975 make public earlier revisions. Shows increased legal restrictions while police continue to disregard the laws with stricter enforcement.

118. Sawatsky, Walter. "Secret Soviet Handbook on Religion." Religion in Communist Lands 4 (1976): 24-34.

119. Simon, Gerhard. Church, State and Opposition in USSR. Translated by Kathleen Matchett. Berkeley: University of California Press, 1974.

A discussion of the pre-revolutionary church situation is followed by post-revolutionary developments, including the recent past, a study of church resistance to pressures of the state and of the underground church, and documents of dissenters. Avoids oversimplifications and does not treat Russian Christians either as Communist spies or as saintly martyrs engaged in a holy war. An outstanding and very crucial book.

120. Spasov, G. Freedom of Religion in the USSR. London: Soviet News, 1951.

A publication of the Soviet Embassy in London.

121. Spinka, Matthew. *The Church in Soviet Russia.* New York: Oxford University Press, 1956.

    Presents the interaction of the Russian Orthodox Church with the Soviet state at the patriarchal level from 1917 to 1955. Post World War II covered in the person of Patriarch Alexei. A sarcastic, critical account which nevertheless contains solid data. The observations are wholly unsympathetic to Patriarch Alexei. Contains useful bibliography.

122. Steeves, Paul D. "Amendment of Soviet Law Concerning Religious Groups." In *Journal of Church and State* 19 (Winter 1977): 37-52.

123. Struve, Nikita. *Christians in Contemporary Russia.* Translated by Lancelot Sheppard and A. Mason from the second rev. and augmented ed. New York: Charles Scribner's Sons, 1967.

    A comprehensive treatment of the role and significance of Christianity in Russia especially from 1917 to the 1960s. Based on primary Russian sources, it is one of the most comprehensive treatments of the subject. Mixes historical, denominational, and thematic approaches. Though claiming complete objectivity, the book shows a distinct Russian Orthodox bias. Six appendices (pp. 343-418) provide documents, lists, and other data useful to scholars.

124. Thrower, James. *Marxist-Leninist "Scientific Atheism" and the Study of Religion and Atheism in the USSR.* Berlin: Mouton Publishers, 1983.

    A *religionswissenschaftlischer* approach to the Soviet Marxist-Leninist approach to the study of religion both in regard to the problematic and methodology of "scientific atheism." Thrower emphasizes the partisan nature of the Soviet study of religion, but allows for some useful insights in regard to the nature of religion even by such antagonistic scholarly work. He points out the fundamental differences between Western and Soviet approaches. A pioneering work. (*See also* 078, 109).

125. Thrower, James. "The Study of Religion in the USSR [nauchnyy ateizm]." *Religion* 13 (April 1983): 113-126.

126. Timasheff, Nicholas S. "Urbanization, Operation Antireligion and the Decline of Religion in the USSR" *The American Slavic and East European Review* 14, no. 2 (April 1955).

127. Walters, Philip. "The Ideas of the Christian Seminar." *Religion in Communist Lands* 9, nos. 3-4 (Fall 1981): 111-119.

    Examines the ideological aspects of people who had been disillusioned with Marxism and so became Christian dissenters.

128. Yakunin, Gleb and Regelson, Lev. *Letters from Moscow: Religion and Human Rights in the USSR.* Ed. by Jane Ellis. Kent: Keston College and San Francisco: H.S. Dakin Company, 1978.

Denunciation of Soviet religious policies and appeals for human rights by two Russian Orthodox dissenters in the form of letters. (*See also* 157).

Russian Orthodox Church

129. Andreyev, Ivan M. *Russia's Catacomb Saints.* Saint Herman of Alaska Press, 1982.

A description of the life and activity of those Russian Christians who refuse to recognize the legitimacy of both the Soviet government and the Moscow Patriarchate from 1917 to the 1980s. (*See also* 131, 169).

130. Bloom, Anthony. "Christian Witness Today in a Socialist Society." *International Review of Missions* 68 (1979): 294-300.

131. Bourdeaux, Michael. "The Black Quinquennium: The Russian Orthodox Church, 1959-1964." *Religion in Communist Lands* 9, Nos. 1-2 (Spring 1981): 18-27.

Summary of Khrushchev's years of repression of the church, especially Russian Orthodoxy.

132. Bourdeaux, Michael. *Patriarch and Prophets: Persecution of the Russian Orthodox Church.* London: George Allen and Unwin Ltd., 1970. Reprint. London: Mowbrays, 1975. New York: Frederick A. Praeger, 1970.

An introduction by the author and a series of loosely related documents: translations from Soviet writings, legal documents, letters, and *samizdats* critical of the *modus vivendi* reached by the Orthodox leadership with the Soviet regime. Documents explaining the stance of the official Church are by Bourdeaux's own admission not well represented in the book. Thus, what aimed at presenting the Patriarch and prophets in creative tension turns into an indictment of the Patriarch. (*See also* 129, 195).

133. Curtiss, John Shelton. *Russian Church and the Soviet State, 1917-1950.* Boston: Little, Brown, and Company, 1953.

The larger segment of the book deals with the period from 1917 to 1928, but the study was extended to include in less detail the period to 1950. Points to inconsistencies of some favors given to the churches and continuations of an antireligious campaign.

134. Dunlop, John B. "Mnogaya leta: Advocate of a Russian Church-Soviet State Concordat." Religion in Communist Lands 11, No. 2 (Summer 1983): 146-160.

A description and critique of one of the few permitted samizdats, an almanach, Mnogaya leta, which considers the long range social developments in the USSR preferable to western influences and advocates cooperation between a conservative Russian Orthodoxy and the government. Some of the writings in Mnogaya leta seem bizzare.

135. Ellis, Jane. "The Christian Committee for the Defense of Believers' Rights in the USSR." Religion in Communist Lands 8, No. 4 (1980): 279-291.

Describes the work of the above mentioned human rights and right to believe group in the USSR from 1976 to 1980.

136. Ellis, Jane. "USSR: The Christian Seminar." Religion in Communist Lands 8, No. 2 (1980): 92-101.

An account of the sharp reprisals against the group "Christian Seminar" consisting of young converts to Orthodoxy who want to meet to discuss religious themes. Article based on samizdats.

137. Fletcher, William C. The Russian Orthodox Church Underground, 1917-1970. London: Oxford University Press, 1971.

Study of the underground Russian Orthodox movements and organizations based on both Soviet official as well as samizdat and western sources. Points out government intervention in the transfer of Uniate churches to the Russian Orthodox Church. Study of various secret religious movements attempting to avoid governmental suppression. A dependable, well written book.

138. Gustafson, Arfred. The Catacomb Church. Jordanville, NY: Holy Trinity Monastery Press. 1960.

139. Hebly, J. A. The Russians and the World Council of Churches. Belfast: Christian Journals Limited, 1978.

As a result of investigating the relationship between the Russian Orthodox Church and the World Council of Churches the author (pp. 129-173) explores the position of the Orthodox Church in Soviet society and points out the reasons for its very limited scope of actions. Scholarly analysis. (See also 064, 158).

140. Hove, B. Van. "Father Dimitri Dudko and the Hope of the Gospel Today," Diakonia 12, No. 3 (1977): 211-224.

Discusses the case of the dissenter priest Dimitri Dudko. (See also 141).

141. "Interview with Father Dmitri Dudko." Worldview 21 (October 1978): 45-48.

Interview with a Russian Orthodox dissenting priest. A reprint. (See also 140).

142. Johansen, Alf. "The Russian Orthodox Church as Reflected in Orthodox and Atheist Publications in the Soviet Union." *Occasional Papers on Religion in Eastern Europe* 3, No. 2 (February 1983): 1-26.

Surveys information on the religious situation in the USSR since 1917 as reflected in Soviet secular and religious publications. Highlights policies of the party regarding religion, atheist propaganda and the reaction of the Patriarchate to the revolution. (See also 109).

143. Johansen, Alf. *Theological Study in the Russian and Bulgarian Orthodox Churches under Communist Rule.* London: Faith Press, 1963.

Johansen, a Danish Lutheran minister, visits and surveys the literature, mostly typescripts of theses and dissertations from the main Orthodox seminaries in Russia and Bulgaria.

144. Konstantinov, Dimitri. *The Crown of Thorns: Russian Orthodox Church in the USSR 1917-1967.* London, Canada: 1979. (See also 145).

145. Konstantinov, Dimitri. *Religious Persecution in USSR.* London, Canada: SBONB, 1965. (See also 145).

146. Meerson-Aksenov, Michael. "The Russian Orthodox Church: 1965-1980." *Religion in Communist Lands* 9, Nos. 3-4 (1981): 101-110.

Charts religious revival among youth, revival of Orthodoxy, rise of dissenters with a religious orientation, and Orthodox ecumenical activity. Considers the period from 1965 to 1980, despite some persecutions and humiliations, to have been a period of strengthening of Orthodoxy.

147. *Metropolitan Nikodim: Peacemaker, Ecumenist, Theologian, Pastor.* Prague: Christian Peace Conference, 1980.

Series of tributes in memoriam of Metropolitan Nikodim of Leningrad and Novgorod by Eastern and Western church leaders. Shows the role of a person responsible for international relations of the Russian Orthodox Church. (See also 161).

148. Moscow Patriarchate. *The Russian Orthodox Church in the Fight for Peace: Decisions, Epistles, Appeals, and Articles 1948-1950.* Moscow: The Moscow Patriarchate, 1950. (See also 154, 155, 156).

149. Nicholas, Metropolitan. *Speeches on Peace: Third Series 1955-1957.* Moscow: The Moscow Patriarchate, 1958.

150. Pitirim, Archbishop of Volokolamsk. *The Orthodox Church in Russia.* Trans. by Michael M. Wolyniec. London: Thames and Hudson, Ltd., 1982.

   Richly illustrated volume published under special arrangement with the Moscow Patriarchate and the Soviet authorities.

151. Pospielovsky, Dimitry. *The Russian Church Under the Soviet Regime 1917-1982.* 2 vols. Crestwood, NY: St. Vladimir's Seminary Press, 1984.

   A comprehensive history of the modern period of the Russian Orthodox Church in the USSR and abroad. Vol. II deals with the period from 1945 to 1982. Deals with church-state relations, the social position and interaction with society on part of the Russian Orthodox Church and with inner church developments such as theology, liturgy, and canon law. Both the official church hierarchy and dissidents receive nuanced treatment. This is book that is likely to become the standard reference on the Russian Orthodox Church in the Soviet period, based on the author's intimate knowledge of the church and society. Both objective and sympathetic treatment of problems and challenges based on a very extensive multilingual bibliography.

152. "Religious Problems in Russia Today." *Pro Mundi Vita* 58 (1976): 2-32. (*See also* 112).

   The Russian Church and the Soviet State, and the ecumenical relations of the Russian Orthodox Church.

153. Romanyuk, Vasyl. *A Voice in the Wilderness.* Wheaton, IL: Society for the Study of Religion under Communism, 1980.

   A collection of *samizdats* of an exiled Ukrainian Orthodox priest who served long imprisonments in the USSR.

154. *The Russian Orthodox Church in the Fight for Peace: Decisions, Epistles, Appeals, and Articles, 1948-1950.* Moscow: Moscow Patriarchate, 1950. (*See also* 148, 155, 156).

155. *The Russian Orthodox Church: Organization, Situation, Activity.* Moscow: Moscow Patriarchate, 1959.

   An illustrated survey of the developments in the church from an official church position which is cautious and maintains that no government pressures or persecutions have been exerted. Emphasizes peace activities of the Russian Orthodox Church. (*See also* 148, 154, 156).

156. Russian Orthodox Eastern Church Patriarchate. *The Russian Orthodox Church: Organization, Situation, Activity.* Moscow: Moscow Patriarchate, 1959.

   Official publication providing a description of the organizational structure of the Russian Orthodox Church. Guarded on political aspects which allows a variety of interpretations. (*See also* 148, 154, 155).

157. Solzhenitsyn, Alexander. *A Lenten Letter to Pimen Patriarch of All Russia*. Trans. by Keith Armes. Minneapolis: Burgess Publishing Company, 1972.

Sharp criticism of acquiescence by the Russian Orthodox hierarchy of oppressive measures which aim at the destruction of religion. Includes an introduction and commentaries by Theofanis Stavrou and Wassilij Alexeev. (See responses in 099, 128).

158. Strogen, William B. *Communist Russia and the Russian Orthodox Church, 1943-1962*. Washington: Catholic University of America Press, 1967.

From chapter 5 onwards the author treats the period since World War II. He analyzes documents and publications, pointing out the method of cooperation and the accomodation of the churches to the purposes of the Soviet state, especially in peace activities. Pp. 117-145 provide texts of Soviet legislation on religious activities. (*See also* 064, 139, 180).

159. Sysyn, Frank E. "The Ukrainian Orthodox Question in the USSR" *Religion in Communist Lands* 11, no. 3 (1983): 251-263.

Historical roots and recent Ukrainian struggles against russification are the main theme of the article. The Russian Orthodox Church denies Ukrainian aspirations despite the fact that church life is more active in the Ukraine than in Russia. (*See also* 170-173, 187).

160. Walters, Philip. "The Russian Orthodox Church, 1945-1959." *Religion in Communist Lands* 8, no. 3 (Fall 1980): 218-224.

Greater tolerance toward the Russian Orthodox Church was manifested during the post-war recovery years by the government, which brought about an upsurge in Church activities. The Church in turn supports foreign policy objectives of the state.

161. Will, James E. "In Commemoration of Metropolitan Nikodim." *Occasional Papers on Religion in Eastern Europe* 3, no. 2 (February 1983): 27-32.

An appraisal of the role of Metropolitan Nikodim in international church relations and to a lesser degree domestically. (*See also* 147).

162. Zernov, Nicolas. *The Russians and Their Church*. London: S.P.C.K., 1968.

The book originally published in 1945 contains only an appendix (pp. 188-191) on the post World War II years.

Eastern Apostolic Churches

163. Calian, Carnegie Samuel. "Soviet Armenia and the Armenian Apostolic Church." *Occasional Papers on Religion in Eastern Europe* 1, no. 2 (1981): 1-8.

    Impressions of Armenian church life by a Protestant leader of Armenian ethnic background. Emphasizes close bond of Armenian nationality with the church. Evenhanded but superficial.

164. Krikorian, Mesrob K. "The Armenian Church in the Soviet Union, 1917-1967." In *Aspects of Religion in the Soviet Union*, edited by R. Marshall, 239-256. Chicago: University of Chicago Press, 1971. (See also 097).

165. Meha, Elie. "The Georgian Orthodox Church." *Aspects of Religion in Soviet Union*, edited by R. Marshall, 223-237. Chicago: University of Chicago Press, 1971. (See also 097).

166. Ogunessyan, Eduard. "The Armenian Church in the USSR." *Religion in Communist Lands* 7 (Winter 1979): 238-242.

    A report of a revival of Armenian church life based on nationalism, the encounter with science, and the search for a basis of morality. Author decries lack of personal faith and stresses nationalism which he credits with greater liberties for the Armenian Apostolic Church than elsewhere in the USSR.

167. Reddaway, Peter. "Georgian Orthodox Church; Corruption and Renewal." *Religion in Communist Lands* 3 (July 1975): 14-23. Reply by D.M. Lang and Others with Rejoinder in *Religion in Communist Lands* 3 (Autumn 1975): 45-51.

Roman Catholic Church

168. Baran, Alexander. "Propaganda's Concern for the Church in Ukraine and Bielorussia." *Sacrae Congregationis de Propaganda Fide*. 2nd ed. by J. Metzler. (1973): 813-826.

169. Bociurkiw, Bohdan R. "Catacomb Church: Ukrainian Catholics in the USSR." *Religion in Communist Lands* 5 (1977): 4-12. (See also 129).

170. Bociurkiw, Bohdan R. "Religion and Nationality in the Contemporary Ukraine." In *Nationalism in the USSR and Eastern Europe*. Edited by George W. Simmonds. Detroit: University of Detroit Press, 1977. (See also 034, 110, 159).

171. Bociurkiw, Bohdan R. "Soviet Religious Policy in the Ukraine in Historical Perspective." <u>Occasional Papers on Religion in Eastern Europe</u> 2, no. 3 (June 1982): 1-21.

Comprehensive review of Soviet religious policies in the Ukraine since the Bolshevik revolution. Analysis of both the constants and the changing features of Soviet policy toward religion. (<u>See also</u> 159).

172. Bociurkiw, Bohdan R. <u>Ukrainian Churches Under Soviet Rule: Two Case Studies.</u> Cambridge: Ukrainian Studies Fund, Harvard University, 1984.

Only the second paper, entitled "The Uniate Church in the Soviet Ukraine: A Case Study in Soviet Church Policy," deals with the post World War II period. Catholics are among the least favorably treated by the Soviet regime. The Western Ukrainian Greek Catholics were forcibly integrated into the Russian Orthodox Church with the assistance of the government. Wealth of data provided. (<u>See also</u> 180, 187).

173. Bociurkiw, Bohdan R. "The Uniate Church in the Soviet Ukraine: A Case Study in Soviet Church Policy." <u>Canadian Slavonic Papers</u> 8 (1965): 89-113.

174. Bourdeaux, Michael. <u>Land of Crosses: The Struggle for Religious Freedom in Lithuania, 1939-1978</u>. Chulmleigh, Devon: Augustine Publishing Company, 1977.

A narrative based to a considerable degree on the <u>samizdat</u> <u>Chronicle of the Lithuanian Catholic Church</u>. Emphasis is on the persecutions of the church. (<u>See also</u> 183, 192).

175. Bourdeaux, Michael. "Religion and Human Rights: The Case of the Soviet Ukraine." <u>Diakonia</u> 16, no. 3 (1981): 262-271.

176. Broun, Janice A. "Catholics in Lithuania." <u>America</u> 142 (January 26, 1980): 56-59.

177. Broun, Janice A. "Latin Catholics in the Soviet Union." <u>America</u> 143 (August 16-23, 1980): 66-70.

178. Dauknys, Pranas. <u>The Resistance of the Catholic Church in Lithuania Against Religious Persecution.</u> Rome: Pontificia Studiorum Universitas A. S. Thoma Aq., 1984.

The Catholic religious liberties movement is described in the context of the close identification between Lithuanian national identity and Catholicism.

179. Dirscherl, Denis, S.J. "The Soviet Destruction of the Greek Catholic Church." <u>Journal of Church and State</u> 12, no. 3 (1970): 421-439.

180. Dunn, Dennis J. <u>The Catholic Church and the Soviet Government, 1939-1949</u>. Boulder, CO: East European Quarterly, 1977.

Provides the history of the incorporation of the Ukrainian Uniates into the Russian Orthodox Church by the Soviet state and by extension, Soviet inspired anti-Catholic policies in other Eastern European states. Pp. 107-237 deal with the post-war period and include the USSR, Poland, Hungary and Czechoslovakia. (See also 158, 172).

181. Dunn, Dennis J. "The Disappearance of the Ukrainian Uniate Church: How and Why?" In Ukrainskiy Istoryk 9, nos. 1-2 (33-34)(1972): 57-65.

182. Dushnyck, Walter. Martyrdom in Ukraine: Russia Denies Religious Freedom. New York: The American Press, n.d.

183. Grazulis, Nijole, ed. and trans. The Chronicle of the Catholic Church in Lithuania, Vol. 1: Underground Journal of Human Rights Violations, nos. 1-9, 1972-74. Chicago: Loyola University Press, 1981.

English translation of underground typescript samizdat publication of The Chronicle of the Catholic Church in Lithuania regarding government abuses of Lithuanian Catholics. Introductory essay on freedom of religion in Lithuania provided by V. Stanley Vardys. Primary source material. (See also 174, 192).

184. Hrynioch, Ivan. "The Destruction of the Ukrainian Catholic Church in the Soviet Union." Prologue 4 (Spring-Summer 1960): 1-51.

A brief, comprehensive study of the demise of the Ukrainian Catholic Church in the USSR.

185. Hvat, Ivan. "The Ukrainian Catholic Church, the Vatican and the Soviet Union during the Pontificate of Pope John Paul II." Religion in Communist Lands 11, no. 3 (1983): 264-280.

Ukrainian Catholic supression, aspirations, underground activities, and attempts at legalization received new impetus under Pope John Paul II.

186. Mydlovsky, Lev. Bolshevist Persecution of Religion and Church in the Ukraine: 1917-1957. 2d rev. ed. London: Ukrainian Publishers, 1962.

187. Mykula, Wolodymyr. The Gun and the Faith: Religion and Church in the Ukraine under the Communist Russian Rule. London: Information Service, 1969.

A survey of Communist attitude toward religion, Soviet suppression of Ukrainian churches, and a brief overview of recent history, especially during the 1960s of the Ukranian Orthodox, Catholic (Eastern Rite), Protestant, Jewish and Muslim religions. Emphasizes persecution. (See also 172).

188. Reynarowych, Roman. "The Catholic Church in the West Ukraine after World War II." Diakonia 4 (1970): 372-387.

189. Sapiets, Marite. "Religion and Nationalism in Lithuania." Religion in Communist Lands 7, no. 2 (Summer 1979): 76-84.

Relationship between Catholicism and Lithuanian nationalism. The recent period based on the Chronicle of the Lithuanian Catholic Church. Strong emphasis on Lithuanian anti-Russian feelings.

190. Savasis, J. The War Against God in Lithuania. New York: Manyland Books Inc., 1966.

The fate of the Roman Catholic Church with brief references to other churches, and the efforts of the government to spread atheism are described based on study of Lithuanian newspaper and periodical reports. It points out the pervasive impact upon the church of the Sovietization of Lithuania. Well documented.

191. Vaitiekunas, Vytaukas. "Genocide Against the Roman Catholic Church in Lithuania." Baltic Review, no. 2/3 (June 1954).

192. Vardys, V. Stanley. The Catholic Church, Dissent, and Nationality in Soviet Lithuania. Boulder: East European Quarterly, 1978. Distributed by Columbia University Press.

Review of the status of the Catholic Church and the tactics and strategy of the Soviet authorities. The dissent, especially Chronicle of the Lithuanian Catholic Church, receives considerable exposure. (See also 071, 183).

193. Vardys, V. Stanley. "Lithuania's Catholic Movement Reappraised." Survey 25, no. 3 (Summer 1980): 49-73.

Vardys characterizes the religious-nationalist Lithuanian dissent movement as a peaceful, public issue oriented protest seeking democratic changes. A well informed, detailed study.

Protestants

194. Bourdeaux, Michael. Faith On Trial in Russia. New York: Harper & Row, Publishers, 1971.

A story of the dissenting initsiativniki, their Council of Churches of the Evangelical Christians and Baptists, and their persecutions documented on the basis of samizdats. Depicts harsh government persecution and heroic believers' response, despite official church leaders' acquiescence to government policies. Biased in favor of the initsiativniki Baptist; attacks frontally the official, registered Protestants. (See also 196, 198, 202, 212).

195. Bourdeaux, Michael. "Reform and Schism." Problems of Communism 16, no. 5 (September-October, 1967): 108-124.

The reform and dissenting movement among Evangelical-Baptists in the USSR as a reaction to the anti-religious policies of the Khrushchev and post-Krushchev period. Parallels in the Russian Orthodox Church are also reviewed. (See also 132).

196. Bourdeaux, Michael. Religious Ferment in Russia: Protestant Opposition to Soviet Religious Policy. London: St. Martin's Press, 1968.

The subtitle of the book delineates the narrow scope of the book; the issue of Reformed Baptists' (Initsiativniki) interaction with the state, their treatment in the press, their relation to the All-Union Council of Evangelical Christians and Baptists on issues of registration, intimidation, and other administrative measures taken against believers as well as their attempts to express protest against such treatment. Large amount of documentation. (See also 194, 198, 202, 212).

197. Duin, Edgar C. "Soviet Lutheranism after the Second World War." Religion in Communist Lands 8, no. 2 (1980): 111-118.

The dispersal of German Lutherans to eastern portions of the USSR and their meager survival is described along with Latvian, Estonian, and Lithuanian Lutheranism in the post-1945 period.

198. Durasoff, Steve. The Russian Protestants: Evangelicals in the Soviet Union: 1944-1964. Rutherford, Madison, Teaneck: Farleigh Dickinson University Press, 1969.

A slightly modified doctoral dissertation traces the history of the Protestants in Russia and the merger of most of the Protestants in 1944. The focus is on inter-Protestant relations but there is a wealth of information on anti-religious propaganda, and state interference with Protestant activities and the relationship of the various Protestant groups with their government. The author is very sympathetic to the Russian evangelicals. (See also 194, 212).

199. Fedorenko, F. Sects, their Faith and Deeds. Moscow: Publishing House of Political Literature, 1965.

200. Hartfelt, Hermann. Irina: A Love Stronger Than Terror. London: Hodder and Stoughton, 1982.

A novel describing the confrontation of some young Baptists with Communist Party leaders in Moscow. The author paints a one-sided, very bleak picture of the position of believers in USSR. (See also 084).

201. Hebly, J. A. "A New Confession of the Evangelical Christian Baptists in the Soviet Union." Occasional Papers on Religion in Eastern Europe 4, no. 1 (January 1984): 1-14.

The social context and influences upon the creation of a new confession by the largest Protestant group in the USSR.

202. Hebly, J. A. *Protestants in Russia*. Translated by John Pott. Belfast: Christian Journals Ltd., 1976.

The present situation of Evangelical Christians and Baptists in the Soviet Union is described in Part II (pp. 87-186) following a historical narrative of the pre-Revolutionary situation. Describes in detail the relationship of the Protestants to the Soviet society, including issues of religious liberty, church-state relations, and evangelism. Dependable scholarly study. (*See also* 194, 198, 212).

203. Kahle, Wilhelm. "Baltic Protestantism." *Religion in Communist Lands* 7, no. 4 (Winter 1979): 220-225.

Explains severe problems affecting Protestants (Lutherans, Baptists and Methodists) in Latvia and Estonia. Increasing Russian settlement produces nationalistic reaction in the historical religious identification with ethnicity.

204. Klibanov, A. I. "The Dissident Denominations in the Past and Today." *Soviet Sociology* 3, no. 4 (1965): 44-60 and in *Sociology in the USSR: Collection of Readings from Soviet Sources*. Edited by Stephen P. Dunn. White Plains, N.Y.: International Arts and Sciences Press, Inc., 1969.

Attempt at a Marxist sociological approach to non-Orthodox religions. Hostile and superficial. A fine example of what passes for scholarship on religion in the USSR. (*See also* 078).

205. Kowalewski, David. "Religious Protest Outcomes: The Soviet Baptist Case." *Review of Religious Research* 22, no. 2 (December 1980): 198-206.

206. Kowalewski, David, and Arthur Greil. "Religious Sectarianism and the Soviet State: The Dynamics of Believer Protest and Regime Response." *Review of Religious Research* 24 (March 1983): 245-260.

207. Mitrokhin, Lev N. "Some Characteristics of the Modern Baptist Movement." *Soviet Sociology* 6 (1967): 53-65.

208. Pollock, John C. *The Faith of the Russian Evangelicals*. New York: John Felsberg, Inc., 1963.

209. Pollock, John C. *The Christians from Siberia*. London: Hodder and Stoughton, 1964.

210. Rowe, Michael. "Soviet Policy Towards Evangelicals." *Religion in Communist Lands* 7 (1979): 4-22.

211. Sawatsky, Walter. "The Reform Baptist Today." *Religion in Communist Lands* 8, no. 1 (1980): 28-38.

Account of the changing situation of the Reform Baptists who demanded total separation of church and state and antagonized the authorities as well as the registered Baptist leaders. Scholarly, documented account. (See also 194).

212. Sawatsky, Walter. *Soviet Evangelicals Since World War II*. Scottsdale, PA: Herald Press, 1981.

    Large portion of the book deals with the Soviet governments' intervention into the church affairs of the various Evangelical religious groups and associations. Close scrutiny is given to both Soviet theory as well as to concrete legislation, and behavior of the government aparatus from the highest to the lowest instances toward religious groups and their reaction to it ranging from being intimidated to martyrdom. Chapters 4, 5, and 11 are most pertinent to issues of church and society. An outstanding, well written, carefully documented, balanced presentations on the subject of the Soviet state and religion. (See also 194, 198, 202).

213. Sawatsky, Walter. "Soviet Evangelicals Today." *Occasional Papers on Religion in Eastern Europe* 4, no. 2 (March 1984): 1-20.

    Circumstances under which the Soviet Evangelicals operate in the 1980's, with few Bibles, growing yet persecuted, trying to keep unity in face of dissent, and seeking peace.

214. Steeves, Paul D. "Baptists as Subversives in the Contemporary Soviet Union." In *God and Caesar: Case Studies in the Relationship Between Christianity and State*. Longview, TX: Conference on Faith and History, 1971.

215. Theodorovich, N. "Mennonites in the USSR" *Bulletin, Institute for the Study of the USSR* 10, no. 1 (October 1968).

216. Toews, John B. *Czars, Soviets and Mennonites*. Newton, Kansas: Faith and Life Press, 1982.

    A presentation of some of the experiences of the non-Slavic Mennonites in Russia from 1789 to 1964. Only a short segment of the book deals with the post World War II period.

217. Wurmbrand, Richard. *The Soviet Saints*. London, 1968.

ALBANIA

218. Bowers, Stephen R. "Church and State in Albania." *Religion in Communist Lands* 6 (Autumn 1978): 148-152.

219. Broun, Janice A. "Albania: The Exile of God." *America* 141 (October 20, 1979): 210-214.

220. Broun, Janice A. "Albania: 'The World's First Atheist State.'" *Christian Century* 98 (March 18, 1981): 303-304, 306-307.

221. Prifti, Peter. "The Current Situation of Religion in Albania." *Occasional Papers on Religion in Eastern Europe* 5, no. 3 (April 1983): 1-6.

   Notes ambiguities arising from Albanian Communist policy to abolish institutional religion.

222. Sadikaj, Dilaver. "The Revolutionary Movement Against Religion in the Sixties." *Albanian Catholic Bulletin* 4, nos. 1-2 (1983): 20-34.

   A translation from an Albanian quarterly *Studime Historike* in which the Marxist author charts measures taken by the government against religion.

223. Sinishta, Gjon. *The Fulfilled Promise*. Santa Clara: self published, 1976.

   The story of the persecutions of the Catholic Church in Albania. Emphasis is on the decade after World War II. Sketchy account in book length form.

224. Sinishta, Gjon. "Grave Violations of Religious Rights in Albania." *Occasional Papers on Religion in Eastern Europe* 3, no. 5 (July 1983): 3-20.

   Repression of religion in Albania described, surveying the fate of Islam, Orthodoxy, and in greater detail, Roman Catholicism.

225. Tonnes, Bernard. "Religious Persecution in Albania." Trans. by G. Ablitt and A. Atkinson. *Religion in Communist Lands* 10, no. 3 (Winter 1982): 242-255.

   Details the composition of the religious populace of Albania prior to abolition of all religion in 1967. Points out the extreme pressure and persecution leveled against all religious communities.

BULGARIA

226. Antonoff, Nicolas and Pundeff, Marin V. *Bulgaria: Churches and Religion*. Washington, D.C., Library of Congress, 1951.

Mid-European Law Project describing the legal position of the churches in Bulgaria after the war. (See also 018, 240, 288, 393).

227. Churches and Religions in the People's Republic of Bulgaria. Sofia: Synodal Publishing House, 1975.

An official publication of the Bulgarian Orthodox Church covering mostly its own history and organization, but also reporting on all other religious groups in the country, including a short chapter on church-state relations. Uncritical, public relations approach.

228. Davis, Lindsey. "Pentecostals in Bulgaria." Religion in Communist Lands 8, no. 4 (1980): 299-304.

Experience of revival among Pentecostals who appear to be the largest and freest of the Protestant churches in Bulgaria, yet are nevertheless harassed by authorities. Well written.

229. Martin, David. The Religious and the Secular. New York: Schocken Books, 1969.

A series of studies in secularization. Chapters 10 and 11 cover secularization processes in Bulgaria. A serious academic study, based on the author's very brief stay in Bulgaria. He presents the attempts and the degree of success of the Bulgarian Communist Party to secularize its country.

230. Popoff, Haralan. I Was a Communist Prisoner. Grand Rapids, MI: Zondervan Publishing House, 1966.

A memoir of the events surrounding the show trial of fifteen Bulgarian Protestant pastors in 1948/49 and subsequent imprisonment written by one of the victims, the Pentecostal pastor Haralan Popoff. Detailed description of inhumane treatment. A bitter personal story. (See also 231, 233, 234, 380-385).

231. Popov, Haralan. Tortured for His Faith. Rev. ed. Grand Rapids: Zondervan Publishing House, 1978.

A second account of persecution by a leading Bulgarian Pentecostal pastor. The author considers Christianity and Communism as eternal enemies. It underscores the persecution and torture of many Bulgarian Christians between 1948 and 1961. A slightly altered version of Popov's I Was a Communist Prisoner. (See also 230).

232. Raikin, Spas T. "The Communists and the Bulgarian Orthodox Church, 1944-48: The Rise and Fall of Exarch Stephan." Religion in Communist Lands 12, no. 3 (Winter 1984).

An analysis of the mysterious resignation of the first Bulgarian Exarch during the time the government undertook to control the churches. (See also 143).

233. *The Trial of the Fifteen Protestant Pastors-Spies*. Sofia: Press Department of the Ministry of Foreign Affairs, 1949.

The English translations of transcripts of the show trial at which the fifteen accused Protestant pastors admitted treasonable and subversive activities against their country. The book illustrates the opposite of its intention, namely the travesty of justice. See Haralan Popoff's *I was a Communist Prisoner* on how the admissions were obtained. (See also 230, 231).

234. *Subversive Activities of the Evangelical Pastors in Bulgaria: Documents*. Sofia: Press Department, Ministry of Foreign Affairs, 1949.

Documents purporting to show treasonable activities of fifteen Protestant ministers (Methodist, Baptist, Congregationalist, and Pentecostalist) leading to a show trial which intimidated all churches in Bulgaria. (See also 233).

CZECHOSLOVAKIA

235. Benda, Vaclav. "Catholicism and Politics," *Religion in Communist Lands* 9, nos. 1-2 (1981): 61-65.

Traces the origins of the present political situation of Catholicism in Czechoslovakia and how it may develop. (See also 180).

236. Bock, Paul. "Church and State in Czechoslovakia." *Occasional Papers on Religion in Eastern Europe* 1, no. 2 (April 1981): 9-23.

With a brief historical survey the article presents the religious developments in Czechoslovakia with a primary focus on the Protestant churches. Shows impact of the Prague Spring, the control of the churches by the state, the internal church activities (e.g. publications), and some church statistics.

237. Capek, Dusan, ed. *Fellowship of Service: Life and Work of Protestant Churches in Czechoslovakia*. Prague: Foreign and Information Department of the Ecumenical Council of Churches in Czechoslovakia, 1961.

A book providing information about all member churches of the Ecumenical Council of Churches in Czechoslovakia, updating materials contained in similar books by Amadeus Molnar (ed.), *Czechoslovak Protestants Today* (1954) and Ludek Broz (ed.), *Yesterday and Today* (1955). First chapter provides theological overview of the Protestant movement by Karol Gabris, followed by chapters on individual churches, church agencies and theological schools. The information in the book is general in scope and accurate. It suffers the limitatious characteristic of official survey books, namely it is uncritical and admits to no real problems or issues facing the churches. (See also 245).

238. Hromádka, Joseph L. <u>Theology Between Yesterday and Tomorrow</u>. Philadelphia: Westminster Press, 1957.

Lectures of Hromádka delivered in 1956 in Canada. One of the books of Hromádka in which he attempted to work out the relationship of Protestant theology to the social order, especially to the socialist one. Important source for understanding the Protestant theological response to socialism in Czechoslovakia and Hungary where Hromádka was an influential thinker. (See also 250).

239. Kalinowska, Milena. "Religious Situation in Czechoslovakia." <u>Religion in Communist Lands</u> 5 (Autumn 1977): 148-157, 157-163.

Emphasis on the situation of the Roman Catholic Church.

240. Kocvara, Stephen and Nosek, Henry. <u>Czechoslovakia: Churches and Religion</u>. New York: Mid-European Studies Center, n.d..

A digest and summary of the legal position of the churches under the Communist regime. (See also 018, 226, 288, 393).

241. Lochman, Jan Milič. <u>Church in a Marxist Society</u>. New York: Harper & Row Publishers, 1970.

A collection of previously published English texts of the Czech theologian Lochman, updated and completed in the optimistic times of the "Prague Spring", somewhat subdued by the events after the Soviet invasion. Study of the responses of the Church of the Czech Brethren, the most influential Protestant group. Theological reflection about church in socialist society in Czechoslovakia by a leading theologian who later immigrated to Switzerland.

242. Nemec, Ludvik. <u>Church and State in Czechoslovakia: Historically, Juridically, and Theologically Documented</u>. New York: Vantage Press, Inc., 1955.

A very comprehensive approach defending the supremacy of the Roman Catholic Church, condemning all movements that directly or indirectly threatened it from Jan Hus to communism. The first one-third of the book deals with pre-1945 matters. The central part of the book is a survey of events from 1945 to 1952 documenting the Communist take-over and the struggle of the Catholic Church, primarily the hierarchy, against the dismantling of its influence, privileges, and encroachments on religious liberty. The last 120 pages are very extensive footnotes, bibliography, and indexes.

243. Rabas, Josef. "The Roman Catholic Church in Czechoslovakia." <u>Occasional Papers on Religion in Eastern Europe</u> 2, no. 2 (September 1982): 1-19.

Describes the exceptionally difficult position of the Roman Catholic Church in Czechoslovakia, detailing the state's oppressive measures, legislation, prohibition of monasticism, the clerical pro-government "peace movement", the relaxation during the "Prague Spring" and later reimposition of violent measures against the Church.

244. Rasker, Albert. "Protestantism in Czechoslovakia." <u>Occasional Papers on Religion in Eastern Europe</u> 3, no. 4 (May 1984): 1-19.

Based on personal experience, the author describes the work of the theologian Josef Hromádka, gives a survey of the main Protestant Churches, Bible translations, and theological work.

245. Salajka, Milan and Svoboda, Jiri, eds. <u>Czech Ecumenical Fellowship</u>. Prague: Ecumenical Council of Churches in the Czech Socialist Republic, 1981.

Survey of denominations and activities of the Ecumenical Council with statistical data and historical background. (<u>See also</u> 237).

246. Tomsky, Alexander. "<u>Modus Moriendi</u> of the Catholic Church in Czechoslovakia." <u>Religion in Communist Lands</u> 10, no. 1 (Spring 1982): 23-39.

The Catholic Church in Czechoslovakia is dying under government pressure and the Vatican <u>Ostpolitik</u> but there are signs of increasing dissent, publication of <u>samizdats</u>, and new hope because of the election of a Polish pope who cares for human rights. A position paper which defends the thesis that only vigorous anti-state dissent can save the soul of the Catholic Church.

247. Tomsky, Alexander. "The Church in Czechoslovakia."<u>International Catholic Review: Communio</u> 8 (Winter 1981): 322-339.

In Slovakia there are signs of a revival of religious life.

248. Tomsky, Alexander. "Pacem in Terris' between Church and State in Czechoslovakia." <u>Religion in Communist Lands</u> 10, no. 3 (Winter 1982): 275-282.

The government's attempt to control the Catholic Church by "peace-priests" failed. Demonstrates government intervention into internal church matters.

249. Vanackere, Hans, ed. "Christians and the Ideological Struggle in Czechoslovakia." <u>Pro Mundi Vita Europe North American Dossier</u> 17 (April 1983): 1-30.

Contrary to laws, the churches' activities are obstructed and freedom of religion denied. Nevertheless, there are signs of Christian renewal. The end to government interference with church work is hoped for.

250. West, Charles. *Communism and the Theologians: Study of an Encounter*. New York: The Macmillan Company, 1958.

    Chapter 2 examines the theology of Joseph Hromadka (238), a Czech Protestant, whose views toward Communism affected the Protestant churches' accomodation to the communist government. Theological study of great perceptiveness.

EAST GERMANY

251. Althausen, Johannes. "Who Do You Say I Am?" *Lutheran World* 24, no. 1 (1977): 65-73.

    Includes discussion of church-state relations in East Germany.

252. Ash, Timothy Garton. "Swords into Ploughshares: The Unofficial 'Peace Movement' and the Churches in East Germany." *Religion in Communist Lands* 11, no. 3 (Winter 1983).

    The role of the independent peace movement in a militarized East German society under the protection of the Protestant Churches. While the political impact is small, the human impact since 1980 is great.

253. Asmus, Ronald D. "The G.D.R. and Martin Luther." *Survey* 28, no. 3 (Fall 1984): 124-156.

    Attempt by the East German government to appropriate all that is progressive in German history. It leads to a reappropriation of Luther with some ramifications for the East German Lutheran and other churches leading to partial rapprochement.

254. Barth, Karl and Hamel, Johannes. *How to Serve God in a Marxist Land*. New York: Association Press, 1959.

    Correspondence between the famous Swiss theologian, Karl Barth and an East German Protestant pastor, Johannes Hamel, wrestling with the issue of the role of the church in East Germany. Theoretically significant theological probing on the dilemmas facing Christians in a socialist country at the height of the Cold War.

255. *Christians and Churches in the GDR*. Berlin-Eastern: Panorama DDR, 1983.

An official survey of basic data about churches in East Germany. Presents the situation in glowing terms. State propaganda material. Some useful factual information. Frequent up-dating and reprinting.

256. Eleutherius (pseud.). "Luther Rebaptized in Marxist Ideology." *Occasional Papers on Religion in Eastern Europe* 3, no. 5 (July 1983): 21-43.

Transition in the East German communist assessment of Luther from traitor to hero (for the 500th anniversary of Luther's birth) and the corresponding impact of such policy shift upon the churches.

257. *The Evangelical Church in Berlin and the Soviet-Zone of Germany*. Witten: Eckart Verlag, 1959.

The Evangelical Churches' struggle against the East German government's attempts to control various facets of their activities is described. A document of early church struggles presented from the churches' perspective.

258. Falcke, Heino. "Place of the Two Kingdom Doctrine in the Life of the Evangelical Churches in the German Democratic Republic." *Lutheran World* 24, no. 1 (1977): 22-31.

259. Hamel, Johannes. *A Christian in East Germany: Writings Gathered from Several Sources*. Trans. by Ruth and Charles West. New York: Association Press, 1960.

Writings of one of the best known East German Protestant pastors and theologians on the role of a Christian in society.

260. Lukens, Nancy. "The Churches in the German Democratic Republic: Notes of an Interested Observer." *Occasional Papers on Religion in Eastern Europe* 2, no. 1 (February 1982): 1-10.

Diversity of perceptions about the self-image of the churches working in a socialist society for the first time as a minority of the population and the changing "social space" of the churches which ceased to be *Volkskirchen*.

261. *Martin Luther and Our Age*. Berlin-East: Panorama DDR, 1980.

Pamphlet recording speeches, lists and pictures from the establishment of the Martin Luther Committee of the GDR. Companion pamphlet, "Thesis Concerning Martin Luther, 1483-1983," gives partial insight into the changing status of Luther in the G.D.R. and the resulting changes for the betterment of the churches' position in society.

262. Maser, Peter. "Suffering from the Church? Aspects of Uneasiness at the Church Basis." *Occasional Papers on Religion in Eastern Europe* 3, no. 1 (January 1983): 20-37.

Points to subtle conflicts within the churches where the church basis may distrust the leadership. The conflict surfaced in the self-immolation of a Protestant minister, Oskar Brusewitz, in 1976. Different unofficial orientations among the clergy are not always publicly heard.

263. Oestreicher, Paul. "The Christian Face of Peace in East Germany." Occasional Papers on Religion in Eastern Europe 4, no. 5 (October 1984): 25-33.

    An insightful perspective on the independent peace activities of the churches in East Germany. The churches' support of young peace activists. (See also 264, 267, 414-419).

264. Ramet, Pedro. "Church and Peace in the G.D.R." Problems of Communism 33, no. 4 (July-August 1984): 44-57.

    An alliance between an independent peace movement, often including unchurched people, and the Protestant Church is described, pointing out that this has not disrupted the basically tolerant policy of the S.E.D. (Communist) party toward the church. Scholarly treatment. (See also 263, 267, 414-419).

265. Röder, Hans-Jürgen. "Churches and Religious Groups in the GDR: Overview in Figures." Occasional Papers on Religion in Eastern Europe 2, no. 1 (February 1982): 11-16.

    Statistics on the Christian churches in East Germany.

266. The Roman Catholic Church in Berlin and in the Soviet Zone of Germany. Berlin: Morus-Verlag, 1959.

    Describes the Roman Catholic Church's struggle against the East German government's attempts to control various aspects of their activities. A document of the early church struggle presenting the church's viewpoint.

267. Sanford, John. The Sword and the Ploughshare. London: Merlin Press and European Nuclear Disarmament, 1983.

    The role of the East German Protestant churches in peacemaking, including the "swords into ploughshares" movement. (See also 263, 264).

268. Schönherr, Albrecht. "The Evangelical Church as a Learning Community in a Changing World." Translated by R.H. Cram. Religious Education 78 (Summer 1983): 398-412.

269. Schottstaedt, Bruno. "The Christian Contribution to the Socialist Way of Life." Mennonite Quarterly Review 55, no. 3 (July 1981): 203-212.

    A working paper on the experiences of the Gossner Mission in the G.D.R. by one of its leaders, who favors supporting the government policies.

270. Solberg, Richard W. *God and Caesar in East Germany; the Conflict of Church and State in East Germany Since 1945*. Foreword by Bishop Otto Dibelius. New York: Macmillan, 1961.

An account of the religious dilemma in East Germany due to pressures of the government upon the churches. A detailed description of the conflict between church and state from 1945 to 1959. Charts the ways in which the communists increasingly repressed the churches and the efforts of various church officials to deal with those pressures and persecutions. Very informative account.

271. Stackhouse, Max L. "The Religious Situation in the German Democratic Republic." *Occasional Papers on Religion in Eastern Europe* 1, no. 1 (February 1981): 1-8.

The impact of Polish events on the church life in East Germany in 1980/81. Church-state relations and the attempts to work out a meaningful existence in a socialist society by Christians, especially Protestants, are analyzed by this first hand observer of the G.D.R. church scene. Sophisticated theological and social analysis.

272. Stolpe, Manfred. "An East German View: The Church, The State and the World." *LWF Marxism & China Study Information Letter* 31 (November 1980).

Discusses Protestant churches' responsibility in East German society and problems arising therefrom. An official GDR church spokesman's moderate theology.

273. Suckut, Siegfried. "From Oppression to Alliance." *Occasional Papers on Religion in Eastern Europe* 3, no. 8 (December 1983):1-9.

Traces the changes in the Christian Democratic Union in the G.D.R. from an opposition party in the 1940's to an unqualified supporter of the government in the 1980's.

274. Swoboda, Jorg. "Bridges Which are Not Too Short: Baptists and Lutherans in the German Democratic Republic." Trans. by E. H. Robertson. *Baptist Quarterly* 30 (1983): 173-182.

275. Vree, Dale. "God's Beloved East Germany." *New Oxford Review* (March 1983): 10-22.

Experiences of an American ex-communist sympathizer and his conversion to Christianity in East Germany. Describes the role of Protestant churches in the G.D.R.

276. Walton, Martin. "The Evangelical Church in the G.D.R.: A Church in Socialism." *Occasional Papers on Religion in Eastern Europe* 4, no. 5 (October 1984): 1-11.

An introductory level survey of the position of the Protestant churches in East Germany and their attempt to come to grips with socialism.

277. Ward, Caroline. "Church and State in East Germany." Postscript by Paul Oestreicher. Religion in Communist Lands 6 (Summer 1978): 89-95.

278. Wensierski, Peter. "Theses on the Role of the Church in the G.D.R." Occasional Papers on Religion in Eastern Europe 3, no.4 (May 1983): 1-19.

Ten theses about the interaction between the Marxist party and the churches in a secularizing society.

279. Williamson, Roger. "East Germany: The Federation of Protestant Churches." Religion in Communist Lands 9, nos. 1-2 (Spring 1981): 6-17.

Traces adjustments of the Protestants during various phases of socialization. The social responsibility of the Federation of Protestant Churches and human rights are examined. Objective, conciliatory, willing to see positive developments.

280. Yoder, Bill. "The Methodist Church in the German Democratic Republic." Occasional Papers on Religion in Eastern Europe 3, no. 8 (December 1983): 11-24.

Traces the history, organization, structure and church-state relations of East German Methodism.

281. Zademach, Wieland. "God's People in Socialism as Exemplified in the G.D.R." Occasional Papers on Religion in Eastern Europe 5, no. 1 (February 1985): 17-30.

Church-state issues since 1949 and the theology of the church in socialism, especially as interpreted by Bishop Krusche.

HUNGARY

282. Aczel, György. "The Socialist State and the Churches." In The New Hungarian Quarterly 18, no. 66 (Summer 1966): 49-62.

A proposal of guidelines for church-state relations by a senior Communist Party official in Hungary which signaled an era of improved church-state relations. A response was written by Bishop Jozsef Cserhati, Roman Catholic bishop of Pecs. (See also 290).

283. András, Emmerich. "The Hungarian Catholic Church in Tension Between Loyalty and Opposition." Occasional Papers on Religion in Eastern Europe 5, no. 2 (April 1985): 1-12.

An examination of the goals of the state and the attempt of the church to find a new form for its activity under the more tolerant yet still restrictive state policies. This is an analysis by a close scholarly observer of the Catholic Church in Hungary.

284. András, Emmerich, "The Hungarian Practice of Christian-Marxist Dialogue." *Occasional Papers on Religion in Eastern Europe* 2, no. 5 (August 1982): 21-25.

Social role and responsibility of Christians, different understandings of the term dialogue, and the dialogical engagement between Hungarian Marxists and Roman Catholics.

285. András, Emmerich. "Basic Characteristics of Hungarian Church Politics." *Occasional Papers on Religion in Eastern Europe* 4, no. 1 (January 1984): 27-44.

A study of Hungarian governmental policies toward the churches by means of analyzing recent speeches of the Secretary of the State Office for Church Affairs, Imre Miklos. Shows improved church-state relations. (See also 303).

286. András, Emeric, and Morel, Julius, eds. *Church in Transition: Hungary's Catholic Church from 1945 to 1982*. Vienna: Hungarian Institute for Sociology of Religion, 1983.

A series of 28 studies written from 1964 to 1982 on the position of the Roman Catholic Church in Hungary with a great amount of material pertaining to church in society and the governments treatment of the Catholic Church. Emphasis on the dynamics of change in that relationship since 1945. Very informed, scholarly analyses.

287. András, Emeric, and Morel, Julius. *Hungarian Catholicism: A Handbook*. Vienna: Hungarian Institute for Sociology of Religion, and Toronto: St. Elizabeth of Hungary Parish, 1983.

A comprehensive resource book containing the history, organization, statistics, publications, legislation, names, and addresses of bishops and other church officials, maps, and so forth. Indispensable library reference material. (See also 180).

288. Bedo, Alexander, and others. *Church and State in Hungary*. (Mid-European Law Project, *Church and State Behind the Iron Curtain: Czechoslovakia, Hungary, Poland, Romania*). New York: Praeger, 1955: 69-157.

Status of churches, laws on churches, and trials of clergy. Brings up to date the Mid-European Law Project, *Hungary, Churches and Religion*. Washington, D.C.: Library of Congress, 1951. (See also 018, 226, 240, 393).

289. Boner, Peter. "Ethical Detente: Marxist-Christian Dialogue in Hungary." *Religion in Communist Lands* 13, no. 1 (Spring 1985): 48-53.

The Hungarian Marxists seem to be replacing "ideological struggle" with "dialogue" in their relationship with Christians. Instead of exchanges of difference of opinion, those in dialogue seem to be seeking consesus in regard to social issues. Boner is reserved and sceptical about the direction of this dialogue.

290. Cserháti, József. "Open Gates." *The New Hungarian Quarterly* 18, no. 67 (Fall 1967): 48-62.

A response by the Roman Catholic bishop of Pecs to Gyorgy Aczel's article "The Socialist State and the Churches" (282) in which Cserhati spells out conditions which would help normalize church-state relations. The two articles reflect the efforts made on both sides to bring about the present improved church-state relations in Hungary.

291. Cusling, George. "Protestantism in Hungary." *Religion in Communist Lands* 10, no. 2 (Fall 1982): 124-132.

An analysis of the slowly declining Protestant Church life with some sociological data provided by Hungarian sociologists.

292. Eibner, John V. "Zoltan Kaldy: A New Way for the Church in Socialism?" *Religion in Communist Lands* 13, no. 1 (Spring 1985): 33-47.

Traces the ecclesiastial and political career of the Lutheran Bishop Kaldy of Hungary who favors rapprochment of the churches and the government. The author charts post World War II church-state developments especially as it involved the Lutherans and points out Kaldy's leadership of the church in fostering pro-socialist policies.

293. Gombos, Gyula. *The Lean Years; a Study of Hungarian Calvinism in Crisis*. New York: Kossuth Foundation, 1960.

Analysis of the developments within the Hungarian Reformed Church after World War II and the method of infiltration of the church by the government.

294. Harsányi, Andrew. "The Reformed Church in Hungary Today." *Occasional Papers on Religion in Eastern Europe* 2, no. 5 (August 1982): 1-20.

A description of the activities of the Hungarian Reformed Church both inside the church and in its relations with the state. Discussion of the meaning and scope of religious freedom or persecutions.

295. Hungarian Government. *Documents on the Mindszenty Case*. Budapest: Athenaeum, 1949.

Pretrial publication of an alleged confesion, letters and other documents aiming at demonstrating the government's charge of high treason and currency violations of Jozsef Cardinal Mindszenty. (*See also* 304-306).

296. Hungarian Government. <u>The Trial Of József Mindszenty</u>. Budapest: Hungarian State Publishing House, 1949.

Excerpts of the English translations of the transcripts of the trial of Cardinal Mindszenty along with claims of freedom of religion in Hungary. A good example of the nature of show trials which were a gross miscarriage of justice. (<u>See also</u> 304-306).

297. Javers, R. "Hungary: Twenty Years Later." <u>Commonweal</u> 103 (1976): 711-716.

298. Kádár, Imre. <u>The Church in the Storm of Time; The History of the Hungarian Reformed Church During the Two World Wars, Revolutions, and Counterrevolutions</u>. Budapest: Bibliotheca, 1958.

A very biased partisan account of the developments within the Hungarian Reformed Church according to the prevalent official view.

299. Kovats, Charles E. "The Path of Church-State Reconciliation in Hungary." In <u>Eastern Europe's Uncertain Future</u>. Edited by Robert R. King and James F. Brown, pp. 301-311. New York: Frederick A. Praeger, 1977.

300. László, Leslie. "The Base Community- A Challenge to the Peaceful Co-existence Between Church and State in Hungary." <u>Occasional Papers on Religion in Eastern Europe</u> 1, no. 6 (November 1981): 1-9.

Points to the sociological need for small, base communities in Hungary, their activities, leadership and goals as well as the opposition to them by both the government and the Roman Catholic Church leadership.

301. László, Leslie. "Religion in a Communist Consumer Society: The Case of Kadar's Hungary." <u>Occasional Papers on Religion in Eastern Europe</u> 1, no. 5 (September 1981): 1-10.

The impact of the government's conciliatory policies toward the churches in the last two decades, the still strong impact of churches upon society, the role of youth, consumerism, and social evils, and the response of the Roman Catholic Church are presented.

302. Medyesy, Laslo M. <u>Evolution of the Socialist "New Man" in Hungary</u>. Vienna: Hungarian Institute for Sociology of Religion, 1980.

Description of attempts to create the "New Human Being" along Marxist lines with primary focus on the educational system and pseudo- religious ceremonies. The first chapter deals with pre-Marxian attempts to shape "the new human being" in Hungary. The last chapter presents a wealth of empirical data. Bibliography primarily in Hungarian.

303. Miklós, Imre and Others. "Hungary: The Forerunner." IDOC Bulletin NS 7 (July 1977): 3-44.

Church and state in Eastern Europe with emphasis on Hungary. Contains responses to the 1976 Dossier Church Within Socialism. (See also 045). Imre Miklós, Secretary of Church Affairs of the Hungarian government writes about "Relations of a New Type," maintaining that a new climate has been achieved in church-state relations. (See also 032, 285).

304. Mindszenty, Cardinal József. Cardinal Mindszenty Speaks: Authorized White Book. Introduction by Ákos Zombory. New York: Longmans Green, 1949.

Cardinal Mindszenty's authorized documentation in case of his arrest, which, indeed, did take place. (See also 295, 296).

305. Mindszenty, Cardinal József. Four Years' Struggle of the Church in Hungary. Edited by C. Hollis. London: Longmans, Green and Co., 1949.

306. Mindszenty, József Cardinal. Memoirs. New York: Macmillan Publishing Company, 1974.

Autobiographical reminescences mostly of the post-war struggle between the Communists and the Catholic Church in Hungary by the rigidly conservative Cardinal Primate. Valuable primary source. Nearly half the book consists of documents supporting Mindszenty's case. (See also 295, 296, 316).

307. Molnár, Thomas. "Church and Society in Communist Hungary." New Oxford Review (November 1984): 8-12.

Random observations on changes in church and society by an exile visiting his native land. Superficial.

308. Patkai, Robert J. "Analysis or Slander?" Religion in Communist Lands 12, no. 2 (Summer 1984): 145-148.

A defense of Vilmos Vajta's theological critique of the Hungarian Lutheran official "theology of diaconia." See Vajta's article below. (See also 314, 315).

309. Polgár, Steven. "A Summary of the Situation of the Hungarian Catholic Church." Religion in Communist Lands 12, no. 1 (Spring 1984): 11-38.

Periodizes the post-1945 period into the Mindszenty years, post-1956 and the Lékai years. The author favors the more confrontational policy of Mindszenty than the accomodations of recent years. Much attention is given to the "basis communities" which are in conflict with the hierarchy which the author interprets as primarily rejecting the hierarchy's accomodationist policies.

310. Shuster, George N. *In Silence I Speak: The Story of Cardinal Mindszenty Today and of Hungary's "New Order"*. New York: Farrar, Straus and Cudahy, 1956.

An account of the life and activities of József Cardinal Mindszenty and the social conditions, especially from 1944 to 1956. A well written narative which, however, paints events in only black and white. As a self-professed anti-totalitarian, Shuster writes an indictment of those not like-minded to Mindszenty rather than a history. (See also 304-306).

311. Tomka, Miklós. "A Balance of Secularization in Hungary." *Social Compass* 28, no. 1 (1981): 25-42.

Reprint of a translation from the Hungarian atheist journal *Világosság*, no. 7 (1979), which also includes selected bibliography of sociological studies on religion in Hungary (pp. 125-141).

312. Tomka, Miklós. "The Religious- Non-Religious Dichotomy as a Social Problem." *A. R. Social Science Religion* 3 (1979): 105-137.

A sociological investigation of the religious-non-religious dichotomy in Hungary.

313. Tóth, Károly. "The Church in Socialism." *Communio Viatorum* 27, nos. 1-2 (1984): 33-45. Also *Occasional Papers on Religion in Eastern Europe* 5, no.2 (April 1985): 19-33.

Theses of the prominent Hungarian Reformed Bishop and President of the Christian Peace Conference on the mode of the church's existence in socialism. Toth is a proponent of adjustments and rapprochement. The article reflects the "official" position of many churches in Eastern Europe.

314. Vajta, Vilmos. "Debatable 'Theology of Diaconia' - Hungarian Example of 'The Church in Socialist Society'." *Occasional Papers on Religion in Eastern Europe* 4, no. 1 (January 1984): 45-60.

Critical examination of the achievements and pitfalls of the Hungarian Lutheran Church's official "Theology of Diaconia" in its relationship with the state. (See also 308, 315).

315. Vajta, Vilmos. "Dispute Over the 'Theology of Diaconia' - The Hungarian Version of 'The Church in Socialist Society'." *Religion in Communist Lands* 12, no. 2 (Summer 1984): 130-142.

A theological critique of the "official" Hungarian Lutheran theology of service which emphasizes the church's cooperation in the building of socialism. (See also 292, 308, 314).

316. Vincent, James T. "Mindszenty Remembered," <u>Problems of Communism</u> 6, no. 6 (November-December 1977): 65-70.

Book review essay of Mindszenty's <u>Memoirs</u>. (<u>See also</u> 306).

POLAND

317. "Christian Churches and Religious Unions in Poland: State as of December 13, 1981." <u>Occasional Papers on Religion in Eastern Europe</u> 3, no.4 (May 1983): 30-36.

Church statistics.

318. "On National and Religious Affiliation." <u>Survey</u> 25, no. 1 (Winter 1980): 195-203.

An anonymous Polish writer's reflections on the increase of identification of religion and nationalism at times when the oppressor is of another faith or atheist. This plays a large role in Polish-Russian relations. (<u>See also</u> 180).

319. "What is Published by the Catholic Press in Poland During the Period of Martial Law?" <u>Occasional Papers on Religion in Eastern Europe</u> 3, no. 6 (September 1983): 18-24.

Survey of main articles published by the Catholic press from December 1981 to May 1982 reprinted from the Christian Social Association's <u>Information Bulletin</u> (Warsaw) (<u>See also</u> 425).

320. Bird, Thomas and Maneli, Mieczyslaw. "The New Turn in Church-State Relations in Poland." <u>Journal of Church and State</u> 24 (Winter 1982): 29-51.

321. Blachnicki, Franciszek. "Theology of Liberation -- In the Spirit." <u>Religion in Communist Lands</u> 12, no. 2 (Summer 1985): 157-167.

The founder of the "Light-Life" movement in the Polish Roman Catholic Church, Rev. Blachnicki, develops an authentic theology of liberation which seeks to provide social and political freedom in Poland by non-violent means. (<u>See also 333, 334</u>)

322. Blit, Lucjan. "Polish Episcopate: Spokesman for Society." <u>Religion in Communist Lands</u> 5 (Summer 1977): 81-84.

Author views the Polish bishops as representatives of society and adds a statement of Polish bishops on pp. 85-87.

323. Borowski, Karol H. "Christians and Marxists in Poland: Dialogue or Conflict." *Occasional Papers on Religion in Eastern Europe* 5, no. 1 (February 1985): 1-13.

Borowski reviews Christian-Marxist relations in Poland and characterizes them as conflictual.

324. Charytanski, Jan. "Contemporary Methods of Faith Transmission in Poland." *Communio* 10 (Spring 1983): 92-100.

325. Chodak, Szymon. "People and the Church Versus the State: The Case of the Roman Catholic Church in Poland." *Occasional Papers on Religion in Eastern Europe* 2, no. 7 (November 1982): 26-54.

Confrontation of the people and the Roman Catholic Church in Poland with the Communist government, the changed social role of the Church and its rise in the esteem of the people. Also describes forms of Polish religiosity, Catholic lay groups, the church policy of the communists and the rise of the moral authority of the church.

326. Heneghan, Thomas E. "The Loyal Opposition: Party Programs and Church Response in Poland." In *Eastern Europe's Uncertain Future*. Edited by Robert R. King and James F. Brown, 286-300. New York: Frederick A. Praeger, 1977.

327. Hruby, Suzanne. "The Church in Poland and Its Political Influence." *Journal of International Affairs* 36, no. 2 (Fall/Winter 1982/83): 317-328.

328. Jeglinski, Piotr, and Tomsky, Alexander. "*Spotkania*: Journal of the Catholic Opposition in Poland." *Religion in Communist Lands* 7 (Spring 1979): 23-28.

329. John Paul II (Karol Wojtila). *Return to Poland: The Collected Speeches of John Paul II*. London: Collins, 1979.

330. Kaminska, Anna. "The Polish Pope and the Polish Catholic Church." *Survey* 24, no. 4 (Fall 1979): 204-222.

An analysis of the attempts to weaken the unity of the Catholic Church by the government and the impact which the election of a Polish pope made. Catholic lay groups and Cardinal Wyszinski's role are examined.

331. Kee, Alistair. "Soft-sell Ideology in Poland: Neither Church nor State Can Control the Outcome of the Country's Spreading Secularization." *Christian Century* 97 (1980): 289-291.

332. Kee, Alistair. "The Study of Religion in Poland." *Religious Studies* 16 (March 1980): 61-67.

333. Keim, Paul. "Light-life: Oases of Renewal." *Occasional Papers on Religion in Eastern Europe* 3, no. 7 (November 1983): 14-30.

Describes renewal movement within the Polish Roman Catholic Church started by Rev. Franciszek Blachnicki which has great impact on youth. The movement also offers non-violent resistance to government interventions. (See also 321, 334).

334. Keim, Paul. "A Polish Strategy for Non-violent Change." Religion in Communist Lands 11, no. 2 (1983): 161-169.

Under the Church's influence, upon Solidarity's apparent defeat, Poles are developing ways to change society non-violently. The best example of this is found in the "Oasis" or "Light-Life" movement which advocates inner liberation without violence. (See also 321, 333).

335. Lenert, P. The Church in Poland. London, 1963.

336. Morawski, Dominik. "The Polish Church and the Government." Survey 26, no. 3 (Summer 1982): 193-197.

The Catholic Church's attempt to mediate the crisis, the government's unreliability, the Church's pro-Solarity position and its desire to save lives by preventing excessive hope among the population.

337. Nowak, Jan. "The Church in Poland." Problems of Communism 31, no. 1 (1982): 1-16.

Resistance of the Catholic Church to Communist subjugation caused allegiance of the masses to the Church. The Church used its influence to defend human rights in society and become mediator of conflicts.

338. Piekarski, Adam. Freedom of Conscience and Religion in Poland. Warsaw: Interpress Publishers, 1979.

339. Piwowarski, Władysław. "Continuity and Change in Polish Popular Religion." In Work and Religion, pp. 57-67. Edited by Gregory Baum. New York: The Seabury Press, 1980.

Characteristics of popular Polish religion are presented singling out elements which persisted at least since World War I and processes of change brought about by changes in family structure, urbanization, ideology, laicization, etc. A sociological study.

340. Poland: Church Facing Socialism. Rome: IDOC International, 1979.

A symposium on various aspects of the interrelationship between church and society in Poland, including such issues as the influence of industrialization on traditional religiosity, Christian-Marxist dialogue, dissent, ecumenical relations, relation between the Catholic Church and the socialist state, and the papal visit. Included is a short section containing documentation and statistics. Varied quality, mostly reprints from works published previously but not easily accessible in the West.

341. Pomian-Srzednicki, Maciej. *Religious Change in Contemporary Poland: Secularization and Politics*. London: Routledge & Kegan Paul, 1982.

   A sociological exploration of signs of vitality or weakness in Polish religiosity using secularization, and its opposite, desecularization as signals of the role of religion in society. The author points out the totalitarian nature of Marxism-Leninism which increases the importance of religion as one of the few, if not the only, form of resisting total Communist Party control.

342. Pospieszalski, Antoni. "Lay Catholic Organizations in Poland." *Survey* 24, no. 4 (Fall 1979): 237 ff.

   PAX, Znak, and other official and more recently unofficial Catholic lay organizations and their role are described.

343. Sharpless, Richard, Lammers, Stephen, and Mojzes, Paul. "Polish Anxieties, Soviet Apprehensions." *Occasional Papers on Religion in Eastern Europe* 1, no. 7 (December 1981): 13-21.

   Impressions from a Christian-Marxist Peace Symposium in Madrid on the religious and social implications of "Solidarity" and church-state relations in the days just before the imposition of martial law in Poland.

344. Sikorska, Grazyna. "'To Kneel Only Before God': Father Jerzy Popieluszko." *Religion in Communist Lands* 12, no. 2 (Summer 1985): 149-156.

   The outspoken criticism of the government and support for the outlawed labor union "Solidarity" by Rev. Popieluszko, with extensive quotes from his sermons are given in this article.

345. Slowacki, Roman. "Catholic Intellectuals and Constitutional Change in Poland." *Religion in Communist Lands* 4 (Autumn 1976): 12-15.

346. Swiecicki, Andrzej. "The Polish Church." *Pro Mundi Vita Europe North America Dossier* 10 (1980): 1-36.

347. Szajkowski, Bogdan. *Next to God...Poland*. New York: St. Martin's Press, 1983.

   Describes the unique identification and interaction between Catholicism and Polish nationalism. Very detailed account of events and documents of the period since 1970 and especially the early 1980s. Special attention given to the role of the church in these critical years, the emergence of "Solidarity," and the failures of the Communist Party.

348. Tomsky, Alexander. *Catholic Poland*. Keston: Keston College, 1982.

349. Tomsky, Alexander. "John Paul II in Poland: Pilgrim of the Holy Spirit." Religion in Communist Lands 7, no. 3 (Fall 1979): 160-165.

   An analysis of the impact of the first papal visit to Poland. Predicts massive consequences. Adulation of the impact of John Paul II upon the Catholic nature of Poland and a rebirth of spirituality worldwide.

350. Tomsky, Alexander. "Poland's Church on the Road to Gdansk." Religion in Communist Lands 9, nos. 1-2 (Spring 1981): 28-39.

   A description of the Catholic Church's firm opposition to the government. The author's thesis is that only Christianity can offer an alternative to totalitarianism and free the people from it. Covers the period from Communist takeover to the election of Karol Wojtila to the papacy and its impact on Poles. A hardline approach which sees every other approach but the formal position of Cardinal Wyszinski as an effort to weaken the church.

351. Walicki, Jerzy. Religious Life in Poland. Warsaw: Interpress Publishers, 1970.

352. De Weydenthal, J. B. "The Pope's Pilgrimage to Poland." Religion in Communist Lands 12, no. 1 (Spring 1984): 69-76.

   Points out the discrepancies between the regime's and the church's assessments of social life during the second papal visit to Poland in 1983.

353. Wielowiejski, A. "Christians and Socialism in Poland," Catholic Mind 77 (June 1979): 38-48.

354. Wierzbianski, B., ed. White Paper on the Persecution of the Church in Poland. London, n.d.

355. Will, James E. "The Church and the Contemporary Social Dynamics in Poland." Occasional Papers on Religion in Eastern Europe 1, no. 2 (April 1981): 1-14.

   Historical background, institutional strength of the Roman Catholic Church, Christian education, access to media, and the church's role in contemporary social change are among topics described with an eye to the situation in 1980.

356. Will, James. "Promise and Peril in Poland." Christian Century 98 (January 28, 1981): 73-77.

   The political and religious situation arising out of the "Solidarity" labor union's impact upon Poland.

357. Will, James. "Reflections on the Role of the Catholic Church in Mediating the Present Crisis in Poland." Occasional Papers on Religion in Eastern Europe 2, no. 6 (September 1982): 20-31.

Investigation of some of the historic associations of Catholicism with Polish nationalism, the social role and teachings of the Catholic Church which makes the church a natural mediator in times of national crises.

358. Williams, George H. *The Mind of John Paul II: Origins of His Thought and Action*. New York: The Seabury Press, 1981.

359. Yoder, Bill. "Poland in Mid-1984." *Occasional Papers on Religion in Eastern Europe* 5, no. 1 (February 1985): 14-16.

    Brief survey of Protestant growth and inter-church relations since the martial law.

360. Zaborowsky, Jan. *The Catholic Church on the Odra and Nysa*. Warsaw: Novum, 1976.

    The role of the Catholic Church in incorporating the western territories.

ROMANIA

361. Antonie, Bishop. "Church and State in Romania." In *Church and State/Opening a New Ecumenical Discussion*, pp. 90-113. Edited by Lukas Vischer. Geneva: WCC, 1978.

    Bishop Antonie comments on church-state relations in Romania.

362. Broun, Janice A. "Catholics in Romania: A History of Survival." *America* 150, no. 18 (1984): 357-361.

    Surveys the fate of both Eastern Rite Catholics (incorporated into the Romanian Orthodox Church) and Latin Rite Catholics (without legal charter) under renewed persecution since 1982. Presents a generally bleak picture and crass government intrusion in church life.

363. Broun, Janice. "The Latin-Rite Roman Catholic Church of Romania." *Religion in Communist Lands* 12, no. 2 (Summer 1984): 168-184.

    Janice Broun charts the many cases of oppression by the Romanian government of the Latin-Rite Catholics, who are ethnically divided and who resist government domination. As in her other surveys of church situations Ms. Broun tends to provide a martyrological, conflictual depiction of the situation. (*See also* 176, 177, 362).

364. Broun, Janice A. "Romania's Churches Behind the Facade of Liberalism." *America* 150 (March 10, 1984): 165-169.

365. Delcroy, P., ed. "The Church in Romania." *Pro Mundi Vita Dossiers* 4 (1978): 1-30.

   Discriminating but sympathetic treatment of the Orthodox Church, Roman Catholic Church, and the Uniate issue.

366. Hitchens, Keith. *Orthodoxy and Nationality*. Cambridge, MA, 1977.

   Deals with the link between Romanian Orthodoxy and nationalism.

367. King, Arthur. "Religion and Rights: A Dissenting Minority as a Social Movement in Romania." *Social Compass* 28, no. 1 (1981): 113-119.

368. Lotz, Denton. "Factors Influencing Baptist Church Growth in Romania." *Occasional Papers on Religion in Eastern Europe* 1, no. 4 (August 1984): 11-15.

   A few social factors contributing to rapid expansion of Baptists in Romania, making it one of the largest Baptist churches in Europe.

369. Mory, Eileen, S.L.G. "Orthodox Monasticism in Romania Today." *Religion in Communist Lands* 8, no. 1 (1980): 22-27.

   The blending of the ancient monastic tradition and everyday Romanian life makes monasticism strong, especially among women. The greater threat to it is Western-type secularism and industrialization than the present political regime.

370. Pope, Earl A. "Church-State Relations in Romania." *Kyrkohistorisk arsskrift 1977*: 291-297.

   Survey of recent developments across denominational lines.

371. Pope, Earl A. "Ecumenism in Eastern Europe: Romanian Style." *East European Quarterly* 13 (Spring 1979): 185-212.

372. Pope, Earl A. "The Romanian Orthodox Church." *Occasional Papers on Religion in Eastern Europe* 1, no. 3 (June 1981): 1-17.

   Describes the religious policies of the Romanian government and the activities of the officially recognized churches, especially the very strong Romanian Orthodox Church, its education, publications and ecumenism.

373. *The Romanian Orthodox Church*. Bucharest: Bible and Orthodox Missionary Institute, 1968.

An official church publication presenting succinctly the history, organization, and mission of the Romanian Orthodox Church. Also includes summary of ecumenical relations of that church. Deals with church-state issues only by inference. Innocuous. Not very helpful. Reprinted periodically. (See also 374).

374. *The Romanian Orthodox Church Yesterday and Today*. Bucharest: Patriarchate, 1979.

Official account similar to 373.

375. Romanian Orthodox Patriarchate, Department of Foreign Relations, ed. *Romanian Orthodox Church News: Fiftieth Anniversary of the Romanian Patriarchate*. 5, no. 4 (1975).

Fiftieth anniversary issue of the Romanian Patriarchate and 90th anniversary of the recognition of the autocephaly of the Romanian Orthodox Church. A compilation of the history, administration, biographies, statistics, ecumenical contacts, and news from various dioceses. Illustrated with photos and maps.

376. Scarfe, Alan. "A Call for Truth: An Appraisal of Romanian Baptist Church-State Relations." *Journal of Church and State* 21 (1979): 431-449.

377. Scarfe, Alan. "Dismantling a Human Rights Movement; a Romanian Solution." *Religion in Communist Lands* 7, no. 3 (Fall 1979): 166-170.

Forced emigration and repression is threatening the Romanian human rights movement. The human rights movement among some Baptists and a few Orthodox priests is charted. Church-state relations in the context of this human rights movement is examined.

378. Scarfe, Alan. "Romanian Baptists and the State." *Religion in Communist Lands* 4 (Summer 1976): 14-20.

379. Villiers, Miranda. "The Romanian Orthodox Church Today." *Religion in Communist Lands* 3 (May/June 1973): 4-7.

A positive assessment of the life of the Orthodox Church, where, despite restrictions, people still uphold the traditions in a massive way.

380. Wurmbrand, Richard. *Christ in the Communist Prisons*. Edited by Charles Foley. New York: Coward-McCann, 1968.

Autobiography of nearly 15 years of imprisonment in Romania, written in the style of an adventure novel. It may not be hard to sift truth from fiction in Wurmbrand's account. A book which is to be used cautiuosly because much of it is self-serving and propagandistic. (See also 230, 231).

381. Wurmbrand, Richard. *God's Underground*. London, 1968.

382. Wurmbrand, Richard. If That Were Christ Would You Give Him Your Blanket?. London, 1970.

383. Wurmbrand, Richard. Sermons in Solitary Confinement. London, 1969.

   A collection of allegedly memorized sermons composed during three years in solitary confinement in Romania. The author admits that many of his meditations are unorthodox, composed under great stress.

384. Wurmbrand, Richard. Tortured for Christ. London, 1967.

   Personal account of persecution by the independent Protestant pastor from Romania who refused to abide by legal restrictions against religion and operated in the underground before arrest and long cruel imprisonment. Author currently lives in the U.S.A.

385. Wurmbrand, Sabina. The Pastor's Wife. Edited by Charles Foley. New York: The John Day Company, 1971.

   A novel-like narrative of experiences by the wife of the controversial Richard Wurmbrand, a persecuted minister from Romania, now living in exile in the U.S.A.

YUGOSLAVIA

386. Alexander, Stella. Church and State in Yugoslavia Since 1945. Cambridge: Cambridge University Press, 1979.

   A detailed documented study of the relationship of the Yugoslav state with the Roman Catholic, Serbian Orthodox, and Macedonian Orthodox churches. The only dependable, comprehensive study of church-state relations charting the various stages of the first thirty years after the Communist ascendance to power.

387. Alexander, Stella. "Church-State Relations in Yugoslavia Since 1967." Religion in Communist Lands 4 (1976): 18-27.

388. Alexander, Stella. "Church-State Relations in Yugoslavia: Recent Developments." Religion in Communist Lands 5 (1977): 238-240.

389. Alexander, Stella. "Religion and National Identity in Yugoslavia." Occasional Papers on Religion in Eastern Europe 3, no. 1 (January 1983): 1-19.

   The divisive role of religion in Yugoslavia with a nation by nation account. Nationalism is a more important factor in regard to religion in Yugoslavia than Marxism-Leninism.

390. Alexander, Stella. "Yugoslavia: New Legislation on the Legal Status of Religious Communities." Religion in Communist Lands 8, no. 2 (1980): 119-124.

Report on the newly enacted legislation on religious communities in all of Yugoslavia's republics with a comparison of provisions. Factual report.

391. Bajsić, Vjekoslav. "The Significance and Problems of Dialogue Today." Journal of Ecumenical Studies 9, no. 1 (1972): 29-39.

The analysis of the nature of Christian-Marxist dialogue in Yugoslavia by a Roman Catholic theologian. A creative thinker's proposal.

392. Cvilc, Christopher. "A Fatima in a Communist Land." Religion in Communist Lands 10, no. 1 (Spring 1982): 4-9.

A reported aparition of the Virgin Mary to some children in Hercegovina evokes mass pilgrimages since 1981 and government reprisals and hostility. Reports of the trials of some Franciscans who were related to these manifestations. The narrative of the events is written clearly and sympathetically.

393. Gjupanović, Fran and Jovanović, George, eds. Churches and Religion, Yugolavia. Mid European Law Project edited by Vladimir Gsovski and Maria Pundeff. New York: Mid-European Studies Center, 1952.

Legal position of the churches in Yugoslavia up to the 1950s. (See also 018, 226, 240, 288).

394. Horak, Josip. "Church, State, and Religious Freedom in Yugoslavia: An Ideological and Constitutional Study." Journal of Church and State 19 (1977): 278-300.

Discusses Marxist concepts of state and religious freedom, church-state relations, and religion in Yugoslav society.

395. Jost, Bishop Radovan. The Church in Yugoslavia. Ljubljana, 1953.

396. Kristo, Jure. "Relations Between the State and the Roman Catholic Church in Croatia, Yugoslavia, in the 1970's and 1980's." Occasional Papers on Religion in Eastern Europe 2, no. 3 (June 1982): 22-33.

Characterizes the relationship between the state and the Roman Catholic Church in Croatia as bad. Points to two factions among Yugoslav Communists in terms of attitudes to religion, of which the more rigid faction dominates politics and escalates attacks upon the church.

397. Manhattan, Avro. Terror Over Yugoslavia; The Threat to Europe. London: Watts, 1953.

The problems of the Roman Catholic Church in the immediate post-war period.

398. Mihevc, J. "Religion in Yugoslavia." Ecumenist 17 (1979): 68-74.

   Introductory narrative of the position of the churches.

399. Mojzes, Paul. "Christian-Marxist Encounter in the Context of a Socialist Society." Journal of Ecumenical Studies 9, no. 1 (1972): 1-28.

   The content and context of Christian-Marxist dialogue in Yugoslavia with stages of the Christian-Marxist encounter from 1945 to 1971. Analysis of the changes in the relationship between religion and the Marxists.

400. Mojzes, Paul. "Marxists and the Churches in Yugoslavia." Occasional Papers on Religion in Eastern Europe 4, no. 2 (March 1984): 21-30.

   Presents the relationship between Marxism and religion in Yugoslavia since World War II. States change in mutual attitudes and relations.

401. Nicoli, Pastor. Persecuted but not Forsaken: The Story of a Church Behind the Iron Curtain. Valley Forge, PA: Judson Press, 1977.

   A simple, fictitious, composite story of the survival of a small non-conformist free church in a rural setting in Yugoslavia in the immediate post-war era of persecution. Much of the harassment is attributed to arbitrary, overzealous, incompetent officials. Nicoli is a pseudonym. Requires critical, cautious reading.

402. O'Brien, Anthony. Archbishop Stepinac, the Man and His Case. Foreword by John C. McQuaid, 2d ed. Dublin: The Standard, 1947.

   A favorable account of Stepinac and his trial.

403. Pattee, Richard. The Case of Cardinal Aloysius Stepinac. Milwaukee: Bruce Publishing Co., 1953.

   Documents and a sympathetic account of Stepinac, including defense documents by an American supporter of Stepinac. (See also 386, 413)

404. Pavlinić, Vladimir. "Church-State Relations in Yugoslavia." Religion in Communist Lands 4 (1976): 40-42.

405. Pogačnik, Jože. "We, Believers Do Not Want To Be Too Exacting." Socialist Thought and Practice 17, no. 4 (1977): 44-51.

   An interview with the Archbishop of Ljubljana regarding the Law on the Legal Status of the Religious Communities and the status of the churches in society in Yugoslavia. Forthright expression of views.

406. Ramet, Pedro. "Catholicism and Politics in Socialist Yugoslavia." Religion in Communist Lands 10, no. 3 (Winter 1982): 256-274.

The author provides a typology of changing relations between the Croatian Roman Catholic Church and the Yugoslav government leading to an uneasy modus vivendi. Though enjoying more freedom than in any other Communist country, there are nevertheless attempts to curb Catholic activities. A well documented study based on many primary sources.

407. Religion in Yugoslavia. Washington: Embassy of the Federal People's Republic of Yugoslavia, 1947.

A report of seven American Protestant clergy who visited Yugoslavia in 1947 on conferences with Catholic, Orthodox, Muslim, and Protestant leaders regarding their institutions. Documentation. Superficial observations illustrate of how well-meaning persons not familiar with the real situation can be deceived.

408. Review of International Affairs, ed. The Legal Status of Religious Communities in Yugoslavia. Belgrade: Medjunarodna Stampa-Interpress, 1967.

Legal documents reflecting the liberalizing attitude toward the churches.

409. Shenck, N. Gerald. "Some Social Expectations on Christians in Yugoslavia with Primary Emphasis on the Protestant Churches." Occasional Papers on Religion in Eastern Europe 1, no. 4 (August 1981): 1-10.

Some effects of socialist experience on religious communities, concepts of the religious sphere and church-state relations and the mutual expectations of church and state. Perceptive analysis.

410. Shepherd, Allen L. "The Christian-Marxist Dialogue in Postwar Yugoslavia." Journal of Church and State 22 (Spring 1980): 315-323.

Brief description of Christian-Marxist relations based on experiences of a seminar for American professors held in Yugoslavia.

411. Vrcan, Srdjan. "Social Class and Religion in Yugoslavia," In Work and Religion, 68-77. Ed. by Gregory Baum. New York: The Seabury Press, 1980.

Research conclusions by Vrcan, a humanistic Marxist sociologist from Yugoslavia, pointing to great diversities in the relationship of religion and society in Yugoslavia. Among important findings is that the proletariat was, after the peasants, the most religious class.

412. Vrcan, Srdjan. "Working-class Commitment to Religion and Society in Yugoslavia," In *C.I.S.R. Actes, 14eme Conference internationale de sociologie des religions* (Lille, 1977): 329-347.

Empirical data showing strong working-class ties to religion and churches in Yugoslavia.

413. Yugoslav Embassy, Washington. *The Case of Archbishop Stepinac*. Washington: Yugoslav Embassy, 1947.

The government's view of the show trial against Alojzije Cardinal Stepinac. (*See also* 386, 403).

MISCELLANEOUS ISSUES

CHRISTIAN PEACE CONFERENCE

414. *My Covenant is Life and Peace: Documents and Information from the Second All-Christian Peace Assembly in Prague (1964).* Prague: International Secretariat of the CPC, n.d..

    Speeches, reports, resolutions, and messages of the 2nd CPC Assembly. Documentation.

415. Roer, Ingo. *Christian Peace Conference: A Place of Ecumenical Peace Work.* Prague: Information Department of the Christian Peace Conference, 1974.

    A survey of the history and relations with the World Council of Churches, peace activity and organization of the Christian Peace Conference. Large amount of statistics. A very informational and balanced account. (See also 263, 264).

416. Roer, Ingo. "The Sixth All-Christian Peace Assembly in 1985 in Prague: In Search of Peace and Justice for All." *Occasional Papers on Religion in Eastern Europe* 5, no. 3 (May 1985): 1-16.

    A sympathetic account of the activities of the Christian Peace Conference leading up to the sixth assembly by a West German clergyman formerly on the Prague office staff. (See also 415).

417. *Statutes of the Christian Peace Conference.* Prague: Christian Peace Conference, n.d.

    English, Russian, German, Spanish, and French texts of the statutes of the Christian Peace Conference based in Prague. No analytic or historical text or introduction added. Useful only to those interested in the organizational structure of the C.P.C.

418. Stefanik, Paul. "The Christian Peace Conference: Propaganda?...or Prophecy?" *Occasional Papers on Religion in Eastern Europe* 5, no. 3 (May 1985): 45-56.

    A general overview of the Christian Peace Conference activities leads the author to the assessment that the propaganda element prevailed over the prophetic element.

419. Urban, Detlef. "A Crisis from the Very Beginning." *Occasional Papers on Religion in Eastern Europe* 5, no. 3 (May 1985): 17-41.

A critical survey of the activities of the Christian Peace Conference from its inception to 1983. Shows shifts in emphasis, both theological and social, during the quarter century of C.P.C.'s activity.

JOURNALS WITH FREQUENT MATERIAL ON RELIGION IN THE USSR AND EASTERN EUROPE

420. **Aksa Bulletin**. Stella Alexander, c/o Keston College, Heathfield Rd., Keston, Kent BR2 6BA, England.

    Extracts from **Aktualnosti Krśćanska Sadašnjost** weekly Catholic news service from Zagreb, Yugoslavia, translated into English. General coverage of USSR and Eastern Europe with emphasis on Yugoslavia. Typed and photocopied without binding. Usually 4-6 pages. Irregular.

421. **Catholic Life in Poland**. Association PAX, Mokotowska 43, Warsaw, Poland.

    Materials published by PAX, a generally pro-government Catholic association, rarely in good standing with the Roman Catholic Church hierarchy.

422. **Christian in the World - ODISS Magazine**. Centre for Documentation and Social Studies, P.O. Box 79, 00-950 Warsaw, Poland.

    Articles and news from an organization of Catholic intellectuals translated from Polish.

423. **Christian Peace Conference**. Jungmannova 9, 110 00 Prague 1, Czechoslovakia.

    Magazine containing short articles, addresses, and speeches relating to the Christian Peace Conference. General issues.

424. **CPC Information**. Information Dept. of CPC, Jungmannova 9, 110 00 Prague 1, Czechoslovakia.

    News service of the Christian Peace Conference, mostly charting meetings and travel of functionaries of the CPC. Newsletter format. The reproduction is of poor quality with no binding.

425. **ChSS Information Bulletin**. The Christian Social Association, Marszalkowska 4, 00-590 Warsaw, Poland.

   Monthly summary of current religious events, press reviews, documentary notes, statistics and occasional articles translated from Polish, usually without commentary. Includes only Polish religious events.

426. **Communio Viatorum**. Theological quarterly pulished by the Ecumenical Institute of the Comenius Theological Faculty. Jungmannova 9, 110 00 Prague 1, Czechoslovakia.

   Usually carries longer theological articles in English, German, and French, many of them written by members of the Comenius Theological School faculty. Journal format.

427. **Czech Ecumenical News**. Ecumenical Council of Churches in the Czech Socialist Republic, Jungmannova 9, 11000 Prague 1, Czechoslovakia.

   Press service on church life in Czechoslovakia, rarely including the Roman Catholic Church. Published occasionally.

428. **Glaube in der 2. Welt.** Bergstrasse 6, Postfach 9, CH-8702 Zollikon, Switzerland.

   Illustrated monthly with significant articles and chronology devoted to church life in the USSR and Eastern Europe. Recently coverage expanded to other communist countries. Only in German. A key resource.

429. **Hungarian Church Press**. Abonyi utca 21, Budapest XIV., Hungary.

   Press service of the Hungarian Protestant churches.

430. **IDOC International.** via S. Maria dell' Anima 30, 00186 Rome, Italy.

   Occasional issues concentrate on the situation of a particulr Eastern European country. Attempt to offer the Western readers translated documents and articles written in the country under study.

431. **Journal of the Moscow Patriarchate**. Moscow Patriarchate, Box 624, Moscow 119435, USSR.

   English edition restricted to chronicling events affecting the Russian Orthodox Church and its context. In addition to describing events, includes texts of comuniques and appeals. Highly controlled information.

432. **Kirche im Sozialismus.** Berliner Arbeitsgemeinschaft fur Kirchliche Publizistik. Bachstrasse 1-2, 1000 Berlin 21.

   A West Berlin Protestant monthly in German devoted almost exclusively to analysis and news of church life in East Germany. A very helpful resource.

433. <u>LWF Marxism and China Information Letter</u>. Lutheran World Federation, Department of Studies, 150 route de Ferney, 1211 Geneva 20, Switzerland.

Occasional newsletter with some analytic articles and shorter interpretations which deal with Eastern Europe and the USSR.

434. <u>News from the Polish Ecumenical Council</u>. ul.Wilowa 1, 00-790 Warsaw, Poland.

News service of the Protestant and Orthodox Churches in Poland.

435. <u>Occasional Papers on Religion in Eastern Europe</u>. c/o Dr. Paul Mojzes, editor, Rosemont College, Rosemont, PA 19010.

A minimum of six issues annually devoted exclusively to various religious issues in the USSR and Eastern Europe. Mostly scholarly studies by authors representing differing perspectives.

436. <u>Problems of Communism</u>. The Superintendent of Documents, U.S. Government Printing Office, Washington, D.C. 20547.

Bi-monthly publication including articles of problems affecting the Communist counties and movements throughout the world. Occasionally includes material on religion in USSR and Eastern Europe.

437. <u>Religion in Communist-Dominated Areas</u>. Rev. Blaho Hruby, 475 Riverside Dr., New York, N.Y. 10115.

Translations of documents from the USSR and Eastern Europe pertaining to religion and shorter commentaries or editorials regarding key documents. Recently expanded to include other Communist dominated areas.

438. <u>Religion in Communist Lands</u>. Keston College, Heathfield Rd., Keston, Kent BR2 6BA, England.

The most comprehensive treatment of religion under Communism, with primary attention to the USSR and Eastern Europe. Scholarly articles, documentation chronicles, book reviews, and photographs. The publisher, Keston College, is the repository of the most significant materials pertaining to religion in Communist countries.

439. <u>Survey</u>. 59 St. Martin's Lane, London WC2N 4LS, England.

Articles on many aspects of life in Eastern Europe and the USSR, mostly of a scholarly nature. Only occasionally articles on religion.

Author Index

This index contains only the primary authors and editors appearing in citations. References to the Introductory Survey are indicated by page number; references to the Bibliographic Survey are by three digit entry number.

-A-

Aczel, György, 282
Agursky, Mikhail, 051
Aksa Bulletin, 420
Alexander, Stella, 386-390
Althausen, Johannes, 251
Anderson, Paul, 001, 052
András, Emmerich, 283-287
Andreev, I.A., 053
Andreyev, Ivan M., 129
Antonie, Bishop, 361
Antonoff, Nicolas, 226
Ash, Timothy Garton, 252
Asmus, Ronald D., 253
Azrael, Jeremy, 002

-B-

Bach, Marcus, 054
Bajsić, Vjekoslav, 391
Baker, Alonzo, 055
Baran, Alexander, 168
Barron, J.B., 003
Barth, Karl, 254
Bastenier, Albert, 004
Bedo, Alexander, 288
Beeson, Trevor, p. 8; 005, 056
Benda, Vaclav, 235
Bennett, John C., 007

Bird, Thomas, 320
Blachnicki, Franciszek, 321
Blanchard, Paul, 007
Blit, Lucjan, 322
Bloom, Anthony, 130
Bociurkiw, Bohdan, 057-059, 169-173
Bock, Paul, 236
Bolshakoff, Serge, 061
Boner, Peter, 289
Borowski, Karol H., 323
Bourdeaux, Michael, 062-066, 131, 174-175, 194-196
Bowers, Stephen R., 218
Braunn, Leopold, 067
Broun, Janice A., 176-177, 219-220, 362-364
Brown, James F., 021

-C-

Calian, Carnegie Samuel, 163
Čapek, Dušan, 237
Catholic Life in Poland, 421
Charytanski, Jan, 324
Chodak, Szymon, 325
"Christian Churches and Religious Unions in Poland: State as of Dec. 13, 1981", 317

Christians and Churches in
    the GDR, 255
Christian in the World, 422
Christian Peace Conference,
    423
The Church Under Communism,
    088
Churches and Religions in
    the Peoples' Republic of
    Bulgaria, 227
Ciszek, Walter, 068
Cockburn, J. Hutchinson, 009
Conquest, Robert, 069
Communio Viatorum, 426
CPC Information, 424
ChSS Information Bulletin,
    425
Cserháti, József, 290
Curtiss, John Shelton, 133
Cusling, George, 291
Cviić, Christopher, 392
Czech Ecumenical News, 427

-D-

Daim, Wilfred, 011
D'Arcy, Martin C., 010
Davis, Lindsey, 228
Dauknys, Pranas, 178
de George, Richard T., 015
de Grunwald, Constantine,
    082-083
DeKoster, Lester, 022
Delcroy, P., 365
DeWeydenthal, J. B., 352
Dirscherl, Denis, 179
Dudko, Dmitri, 141
Duin, Edgar C., 197
Dunlop, John B., 134
Dunn, Dennis J., 012,
    070-073, 180
Durasoff, Steve, 198
Dushnyck, Walter, 182

-E-

Eibner, John V., 292
Eleutherius, 256
Elizando, Virgil, 016
Ellis, Jane, 135-136
The Evangelical Church in
    Berlin and the Soviet
    Zone of Germany, 257
Everett, Glenn D., 103

-F-

Falcke, Heino, 258
Fedorenko, F., 199

Feinstein, Stephen, 074
Fletcher, William, 075-079,
    085, 137

-G-

Galter, Albert, 014
Gjupanović, Fran, 393
Glaube in der 2. Welt,
    428
Glazov, V., 080
Gombós, Gyula, 293
Gossman, Joan Delaney, 081
Grazulis, Nijole, 183
Greincher, Norbert, 016
Grossu, Sergiu, 017
Gsovski, Vladimir, 018
Gustafson, Arfred, 138

-H-

Hamel, Johannes, 254, 259
Harsányi, Andrew, 294
Hartfeld, Hermann, 084, 200
Hayward, Max, 085
Hebly, J.A., 019, 064, 139,
    201-202
Heneghan, Thomas E., 326
Hitchens, Keith, 366
Horak, Josip, 394
Hove, B. Van, 140
Hromádka, Joseph L., pp. 6,
    10; 238
Hruby, Suzanne, 327
Hrynioch, Ivan, 184
Hungarian Church Press,
    429
Hungarian Government, 295,
    296
Hutten, Kurt, 020
Hvat, Ivan, 185

-I-

IDOC International, 430
Inkeles, Alex, 086
Ivanov, Boris, 087

-J-

Javers, R., 297
Jeglinski, Piotr, 328
Johansen, Alf, 142-143
John Paul II, 329
Jost, Bishop Radovan, 395
Journal of the Moscow
    Patriarchate, 431
Jovanović, George, 393

-K-

Kádár, Imre, 298
Kahle, Wilhelm, 203
Kalinowska, Milena, 239
Kaminska, Anna, 330
Kee, Alistair, 331-332
Keim, Paul, 333-334
King, Arthur, 367
King, Robert R., 021
Kirche in Sozialismus, 432
Klibanov, A. I., 204
Kline, George, 088
Kocvara, Stephen, 240
Kolarz, Walter, 089
Konstantinov, Dimitri, 090, 144-145
Kovats, Charles E., 299
Kowalewski, David, 091, 205-206
Krikorian, Mesrob K., 164
Kristo, Jure, 396
Kuroyedov, Vladimir, 092
Kuzmič, Peter, 023

-L-

Lammers, Stephen, 343
Lane, Christel, 093-094
László, Leslie, 300-301
Lawrence, John, 096
The Legal Status of Religious Communities in Yugoslavia, 408
Lenert, P., 355
Levintin-Krasnov, Anatoli, 095
Lochman, Jan Milič, 241
Lotz, Denton, 368
Luchterhandt, Otto, 024
Lukens, Nancy, 260
Lutheran World Federation, 013
LWF Marxism and China Information Letter, 433

-M-

MacEoin, Gary, 026
Manelli, Mieczyslaw, 320
Manhattan, Avro, 397
Markham, R.H., 027
Marshall, Richard, 097
Martin, David, 229
Martin Luther and Our Age, 261
Maser, Peter, 262
Medlin, William, 098
Medyesy, Laslo M., 302

Meerson-Aksenov, Michael, 099, 146
Meha, Elie, 165
Melish, William Howard, 100
Mihevc, J., 398
Miklós, Imre, 303
Mindszenty, Cardinal József, p. 6; 304-306
Mitrokhin, Lev N., 028, 207
Mojzes, Paul, 029-030, 032 343, 399-400
Molnár, Thomas, 307
Morawski, Dominik, 336
Morel, Julius, 286-287
Mory, Eileen, 369
Moscow Patriarchate, 148, 154-155
Murvar, Vatro, 101
My Covenent is Life and Peace, 41
Mydlovsky, Lev, 186
Mykula, Wolodymyr, 187

-N-

Nemec, Ludvik, 242
Newton, Louie, 102
News from the Polish Ecumenical Council, 434
Nicholas, Metropolitan, 149
Nicoli, Pastor, 401
Nikodim, Metropolitan, 147
Noble, John, 103
Nosek, Henry, 240
Nowak, Jan, 337

-O-

O'Brien, Anthony, 402
Occasional Papers on Religion in Eastern Europe, 435
Oestreicher, Paul, 263
Ogunessyan, Edward, 166
"On National and Religious Affiliation", 318

-P-

Paassen, Pierre Van, 104
Pankhurst, Jerry, 105-107
Parson, Howard, 108
Patee, Richard, 403
Patkai, Robert J., 308
Pavlinić, Vladimir, 404
Peachey, Paul, 033
Piekarski, Adam, 338
Pitirim, Archbishop of Volokolamsk, 150

Piwowarski, Władysław, 339
Pogačnik, Jože, 405
Poland: Church Facing Socialism, 340
Polgar, Steven, 309
Pollock, John C., 208-209
Pomian-Srzednicki, Maciej, 341
Pope, Earl A., 370-372
Popoff, Haralan, p. 8; 230, 231
Pospielovsky, Dimitry, 151
Pospieszalski, Antoni, 342
Powell, David, 109
Prifti, Peter, 221
Problems of Communism, 436
Pundeff, Marin V., 226

-R-

Rabas, Josef, 243
Raikin, Spas T., 232
Ramet, Pedro, 034, 110, 264, 406
Rasker, Albert, 244
Reddaway, Peter, 167
Regelson, Lev, 128
"Religion and Churches Function in Socialist Societies", 035
Religion In Communist-Dominated Areas, 437
Religion in Communist Lands, 438
"Religion in the USSR", 111
Religion in Yugoslavia, 407
"Religious Problems in Russia Today", 112, 152
Review of International Affairs, ed., 408
Reynarowych, Roman, 188
Röder, Hans-Jürgen, 265
Roer, Ingo, 114, 415-416
Rowe, Michael, 062, 210
The Roman Catholic Church in Berlin and in the Soviet Zone of Germany, 266
Romanian Orthodox Patriarchate, Dept. of Foreign Relations, 373-375
Romanyuk, Vasyl, 036, 153
Roshchin, Boris, 115
Roter, Zdenko, p. 23; 037
Rothenberg, Joshua, 116
Runciman, Steven, 038
Russian Orthodox Church Patriarchate, 154-156

-S-

Sadikaj, Dilaver, 222
Salajka, Milan, 245
Sanford, John, 267
Sapiets, Marite, 189
Savasis, J., 190
Sawatsky, Walter, 039, 117-118, 211-213
Scanlan, James P., 015
Scarfe, Alan, 113, 376-378
Schönherr, Albrecht, 268
Schottstaedt, Bruno, 269
Second All-Christian Assembly Documents, 414
Sharpless, Richard, 343
Shenck, N. Gerald, 409
Shepherd, Allen L., 410
Shragin, Boris, 099
Shuster, George, 040, 310
Sikorska, Grazyna, 344
Simon, Gerhard, 119
Sinishta, Gjon, 223, 224
Slowacki, Roman, 345
Solberg, Rochard W., 270
Solyom-Fekete, William, 041
Solzhenitsyn, Alexander, p. 14; 157
Spasov, G., 120
Spinka, Matthew, 121
Stackhouse, Max L., 271
Statutes of the Christian Peace Conference, 417
Steeves, Paul, 122, 214
Stehle, Hansjakob, 042
Stefanik, Paul, 418
Stolpe, Manfred, 272
Strogen, William B., 158
Strover, Anthony J., 079
Struve, Nikita, 123
Subversive Activities of the Evangelical Pastors in Bulgaria: Documents, 234
Suckut, Siegfried, 273
Survey, 439
Svoboda, Jiri, 245
Swiecicki, Andrzej, 346
Swoboda, Jorg, 274
Sysyn, Frank E., 159
Szajkowski, Bogdan, 347

-T-

Theodorovich, N., 215
The Trial of the Fifteen Protestant Pastor-Spies, 233

Thrower, James, 124-125
Timasheff, Nicholas, 126
Tobias, Robert, 043
Toews, John B., 216
Tomka, Miklós, 311-312
Tomsky, Alexander, 246-248, 328, 348-350
Tonnes, Bernard, 225
Tóth, Károly, 313

-U-

Udy, James, 044
Urban, Detlef, 419

-V-

Vaitiekunas, Vytaukas, 191
Vajta, Vilmos, 314-315
Vardys, V. Stanley, 192-193
Vanackere, Hans, 249
Villiers, Miranda, 379
Vincent, James T., 316
Voss, Eugen, 064
Vrcan, Srdjan, p. 23; 411-412
Vree, Dale, 275

-W-

Waddams, H. M., 003
Walicki, Jerzy, 351
Walters, Philip, 046, 127, 169
Walton, Martin, 276
Ward, Caroline, 277
Weingartner, Erich, 045
Wensierski, Peter, 278
West, Charles, 250
"What is Published by the Catholic Press in Poland During the Period of National Law?", 319
Wielowiejski, A., 353
Wierzbianski, B., 354
Wild, Georg, 047
Will, James E., 161, 355-357
Williams, George H., 358
Williamson, Roger, 279
Wojtiła, Karol, 329
Wurmbrand, Richard, p. 8; 217, 380-384
Wurmbrand, Sabina, 385

-Y-

Yoder, Bill, 280, 359
Yakunin, Gleb, 128
Yugoslav Embassy, Washington, 413

Yule, Robert M., 048

-Z-

Zaborowsky, Jan, 360
Zademach, Wieland, 049, 281
Zernov, Nicolas, 164

Title Index

The references in this index are to the citation number of entries. Book titles are underlined, articles are in quotations. Journals listed in separate "Miscellaneous Issues" section are also included.

-A-

Aksa Bulletin, 420
"Albania: The Exile of God," 219
"Albania: 'The World's First Atheist State'," 220
"Amendment of Soviet Law Concerning Religious Groups," 122
An American Churchman in the Soviet Union, 102
"Analysis of Slander," 308
Anti-religious Propaganda in the Soviet Union: A Study of Mass Persuasion, 109
Archbishop Stepinac, the Man and His Case, 402
"The Armenian Church in the Soviet Union, 1917-1967," 164
"The Armenian Church in the USSR," 166
Aspects of Religion in the Soviet Union, 1917-1967, 097
"The Attitude to Religion in the New Russian Literature," 051

-B-

"A Balance of Secularization in Hungary," 311
"Baltic Protestantism," 203
"Baptists as Subversives in the Contemporary Soviet Union," 214
"The Base Community-A Challenge to the Peaceful Co-existence Between Church and State in Hungary," 300
"Basic Characteristics of Hungarian Church Politics," 285
"The Black Quinquennium: The Russian Orthodox Church, 1959-1957," 131
Bolshevist Persecution of Religion and Church in the Ukraine; 1917-1957, 186
"Bridges Which are Not too Short: Baptists and Lutherans in the German Democratic Republic," 274
Bulgaria; Churches and Religion, 226

Title Index 97

-C-

"A Call for Truth: An Appraisal of Romanian Baptist Church-State Relations," 376
Cardinal Mindszenty Speaks: Authorized White Book, 304
The Case of Archbishop Stepinac, 413
The Catacomb Church, 138
"Catacomb Church: Ukrainian Catholics in the USSR," 169
The Catholic Church and the Soviet Government, 1939-1949, 180
The Catholic Church, Dissent, and Nationality in Soviet Lithuania, 192
"The Catholic Church in the West Ukraine after World War II," 188
The Catholic Church on the Odra and Nysa, 360
"Catholic Intellectuals and Constitutional Change in Poland," 345
Catholic Life in Poland, 421
Catholic Poland, 348
"Catholics in Lithuania," 176
"Catholics in Romania: A History of Survival," 362
"Catholicism and Politics," 235
"Catholicism and Politics in Socialist Yugoslavia," 406
The CCDBR Documents: Christian Committee for the Defense of Believers-Rights in the USSR, 113
"Christian Churches and Religious Unions in Poland: State as of Dec. 31, 1981," 317
"The Christian Committee for the Defense of Believer's Rights in the USSR," 135
"The Christian Contribution to the Socialist Way of Life," 269
"The Christian Face of Peace in East Germany," 263
A Christian in East Germany: Writings Gathered from Several Sources, 259
Christian in the World-ODISS Magazine, 422
Christianity and Communism Today, 006
Christianity in the Soviet Union, 108
Christianity in the Soviet Union: An Annotated Bibliography and List of Articles, Works in English, 075
Christian-Marxist Dialogue in Eastern Europe, 029
"Christian-Marxist Dialogue in Eastern Europe: 1945-1980," 030
"The Christian-Marxist Dialogue in Postwar Yugoslavia," 410
"Christian-Marxist Encounter in the Context of a Socialist Society," 399
Christian Peace Conference, 423
Christian Peace Conference: A Place of Ecumenical Peace Work, 415
"The Christian Peace Conference: Propaganda?...or Prophecy?," 418
Christian Religion in the Soviet Union: A Sociological Study, 093
Christians and Churches in Socialist Countries, 044
Christians and Churches in the GDR, 255
"Christians and Marxists in Poland: Dialogue or Conflict," 323
"Christians and Socialism in Poland," 353
"Christians and the Ideological Struggle in Czechoslovakia," 249
The Christians from Siberia, 209
Christians in Contemporary Russia, 123
"Christians in Eastern Europe: A Decade of Aspirations and Frustrations," 046
"Christians Witness Today in a Socialist Society," 130
Christ in the Communist Prisons, 380
The Chronicle of the Catholic Church in Lithuania, Vol. 1: Underground Journal of Human Rights Violations, Nos. 1-9, 1972-1974, 183
ChSS Information Bulletin, 425
"Church and Society in Communist Hungary," 307

"Church and Peace in the GDR," 264
Church and Religion in the USSR, 092
"Church and State in Albania," 218
Church and State Behind the Iron Curtain, 018
Church and State in Czechoslovakia: Historically, Juridically, and Theologically Documented, 242
"Church and State in East Germany," 277
"Church and State in Czechoslovakia," 236
Church and State in Hungary, 288
"Church and State in Romania," 361
Church and State in Yugoslavia Since 1945, 386
The Church and State Under Communism: A Special Study, 041
"The Church and the Contemporary Social Dynamics in Poland," 355
"Churches and Religious Groups in the GDR," 265
Churches and Religion, Yugoslavia, 393
Churches and Religion in the People's Republic of Bulgaria, 227
"Churches in Eastern Europe: Three Models of Church-State Relations and Their Relevance for the Ecumenical Movement," 019
Churches in Socialist Societies in Eastern Europe, 016
"The Churches in the German Democratic Republic: Notes of an Interested Observer," 260
The Churches in the Soviet Union, 082
Church in a Marxist Society, 241
"The Church in Czechoslovakia," 247
The Church in Poland, 335
"The Church in Poland," 337
"The Church in Poland and Its Political Influence," 327
"The Church in Romania," 365
"The Church in Socialism," 313

The Church in Soviet Russia, 121
The Church in the Storm of Time: The History of the Hungarian Reformed Church During the Two World Wars, Revolutions, and Counterrevolutions, 298
"The Church in the Soviet Ukraine: A Case Study in Soviet Church Policy," 173
The Church in Today's Catacombs, 017
Church in Transition: Hungary's Catholic Church from 1945-1982, 286
The Church in Yugoslavia, 395
Church, State, and Opposition in USSR, 119
"Church-State, and Religious Freedom in Yugoslavia: An Ideological and Constitutional Study," 394
"Church-State Relations in Romania," 370
"Church-State Relations in Yugoslavia," 404
"Church-State Relations in Yugoslavia: Recent Developments," 388
"Church-State Relations in Yugoslavia Since 1967," 387
"Church-State Relations in the USSR," 057
The Church Under Communism, 008
Church Within Socialism, 045
"In Commemoration of Metropolitan Nikodim," 161
Communio Viatorum, 426
Communism and Christian Faith, 022
Communism and Christianity, 010
Communism and the Churches: A Documentation, 003
Communism and the Theologians: A Study of an Encounter, 250
Communism, Democracy and Catholic Power, 007
"Communism, Religion and the Churches," 002
"The Communists and the Bulgarian Orthodox Church, 1944-48: The Rise of Exarch Stephan," 232
Communist-Christian Encounter in East Europe, 043

Communists Crush Churches in Eastern Europe, 027
Communist Russia and the Russian Orthodox Church 1943-1962, 158
The Communist War on Religion, 026
"Contemporary Methods of Faith Transmission in Poland," 324
"Continuity and Change in Polish Popular Religion," 339
CPC Information, 424
"A Crisis from the Very Beginning," 419
A Crown of Thorns: Russian Orthodox Church in the USSR 1917-1967, 144
"The Current Situation of Religion in Albania," 221
Czars, Soviets and Mennonites, 216
Czech Ecumenical Fellowship, 245
Czech Ecumenical News, 427
Czechoslovakia: Churches and Religion, 240

-D-

"Debatable 'Theology of Diaconia' -Hungarian Example of 'The Church in Socialist Society?'", 314
"The Destruction of the Ukrainian Catholic Church in the Soviet Union," 184
"On 'Dialogue' Between Marxists and Christians," 028
Discretion and Valour: Religious Conditions in Russia and Eastern Europe, p.7; 005
"Dismantling a Human Rights Movement; A Romanian Solution," 377
"Dispute Over the 'Theology of Diaconia'-The Hungarian Version of 'The Church in a Socialist Society'," 315
"The Dissappearance of the Ukrainian Uniate Church: How and Why?," 181
"The Dissident Denominations in the Past and Today," 204
Documents on the Mindszenty Case, 295

-E-

Eastern Europe's Uncertain Future, 021
Eastern Politics of the Vatican, 1917-1979, 042
"An East German View: The Church, the State and the World," 272
"East Germany: The Federation of Protestant Churches," 279
"Ecumenism in Eastern Europe: Romanian Style," 371
The Encounter of the Church with Movements of Social Change in Various Cultural Contexts, 013
"Ethical Detente: Marxist-Christian Dialogue in Hungary," 289
"The Evangelical Church as a Learning Community in a Changing World," 268
The Evangelical Church in Berlin and the Soviet-Zone of Germany, 257
"The Evangelical Church in the GDR: A Church in Socialism," 276
"Evangelical Witness in Eastern Europe," 023
Evolution of the Socialist "New Man" in Hungary, 302

-F-

"Factors Influencing Baptists Church Growth in Romania," 368
Faith Despite the KGB, 084
The Faith of the Russian Evangelicals, 208
Faith on Trial in Russia, 194
"A Fatima in a Communist Land," 392
"Father Dimitri Dudko and the Hope of the Gospel Today," 140
Fellowship of Service: Life and Work of Protestant Churches in Czechoslovakia, 237
"The 'Fifth International?': Dissidents in Eastern Europe," 049-050
Freedom of Conscience and Religion in Poland, 338
Freedom of Religion in the USSR, 120
Four Years' Struggle of the Church in Hungary, 305

The Fulfilled Promise, 223

-G-

"The GDR and Martin Luther,"253
"Genocide Against the Roman Catholic Church in Lithuania," 191
"The Georgian Orthodox Church," 165
"Georgian Orthodox Church; Corruption and Renewal," 167
Glaube in der 2. Welt, 428
God and Caesar in East Germany: The Conflict of Church and State in East Germany Since 1945, 270
God and the Soviets, 054, 083
"God's Beloved East Germany," 275
"God's People in Socialism as Exemplified in the GDR," 281
God's Underground, 381
"Grave Violations of Religious Rights in Albania," 224
The Gun and the Faith: Religion and Church in the Ukraine Under the Communist Russian Rule, 187

-H-

How to Serve God in a Marxist Land, 254
"The Hungarian Catholic Church in Tension Between Loyalty and Opposition," 283
Hungarian Catholicism: A Handbook, 287
Hungarian Church Press, 429
"The Hungarian Practice of Christian-Marxist Dialogue," 284
"Hungary: The Forerunner," 303
"Hungary: Twenty Years Later," 297
"Hypotheses on the Nationalities Factor in Soviet Religious Policy," 110

-I-

"The Ideas of the Christian Seminar," 127
IDOC International, 430
I Found God in Soviet Russia, 103
If That Were Christ Would You Give Him Your Blanket?, 382

"Impact of the Eastern European Churches Upon Their Own Societies," 031
"The Importance of Religion in the Soviet Rural Community," 073
"Interview with Father Dimitri Dudko," 141
Irina: A Love Stronger Than Terror, 200
Iron Curtain Christians: The Church in Communist Countries Today, 020
I Was a Communist Prisoner, 230

-J-

"John Paul II in Poland: Pilgrim of the Holy Spirit," 349
Journal of the Moscow Patriarchate, 431

-K-

Kirche im Sozialismus, 432
"'To Kneel Only Before God': Father Jerzy Popieluszko," 344

-L-

Land of Crosses: The Struggle for Religious Freedom in Lithuania, 1939-1978, 174
"Latin Catholics in the Soviet Union," 177
"The Latin-Rite Roman Catholic Church of Romania," 363
"Lay Catholic Organizations in Poland," 342
"Leadership of Anti-religious Propaganda in the Soviet Union," 081
The Lean Years: A Study of Hungarian Calvinism in Crisis, 293
The Legal Status of Religious Communities in Yugoslavia, 408
A Lenten Letter to Pimen Patriarch of all Russia, 157
Letters from Moscow: Religion and Human Rights in the USSR, 128
"Light-Life: Oases of Renewal," 333

"Lithuania's Catholic Movement Reappraised," 193
"The Loyal Opposition: Party Programs and Church Response in Poland," 326
"Luther Rebaptized in Marxist Ideology," 256
LWF Marxism and China Information Letter, 433

-M-

Martin Luther and Our Age, 261
Martyrdom in Ukraine: Russia Denies Religious Freedom, 182
"Marxists and the Church in Yugoslavia," 400
Marxism and Religion in Eastern Europe, 015
Marxist-Leninist "Scientific Atheism" and the Study of Religion and Atheism in the USSR, 124
"A Marxist View of Christianity," 037
May One Believe in Russia?: Violations of Religious Liberty in the Soviet Union, 062
Memoirs, 306
"Mennonites in the USSR," 215
"The Methodist Church in the German Democratic Republic," 280
Metropolitan Nikodim: Peacemaker, Ecumenist, Theologian, Pastor, 147
The Mind of John Paul II: Origins of His Thought and Action, 358
"Mindszenty Remembered," 316
"Modus Moriendi of the Catholic Church in Czechoslovakia," 246
"Mnogaya Leta: Advocate of a Russian Church-Soviet State Concordat," 134
My Covenant in Life and Peace. Documents and Information from the Second All-Christian Peace Assembly in Prague, 414

-N-

"On National and Religious Affiliation," 318

"A New Confession of the Evangelical Christian Baptists in the Soviet Union," 201
News from the Polish Ecumenical Council, 434
"The Soviet Law on Religion," 117
"New Tendencies in State Policy Towards the Religious Groups in European Socialist Countries," 114
"The New Turn in Church-State Relations in Poland," 320
Next to God...Poland, 347

-O-

"Observations on Religion and Atheism in Soviet Society," 096
Occasional Papers on Religion in Eastern Europe, 435
"Open Gates," 290
Opium of the People: The Christian Religion in the USSR, 063
"From Oppression to Alliance," 273
The Orthodox and the Baptists in the USSR: Resources for the Survival of the Ideologically Defined Deviance, 105
The Orthodox Church in Russia, 150
The Orthodox Churches and the Secular State, 038
"Orthodox Monasticism in Romania Today," 369
Orthodoxy and Nationality, 366

-P-

"Pacem in Terris' Between Church and State in Czechoslovakia," 248
The Pastor's Wife, 385
"The Path of Church-State Reconciliation in Hungary," 299
Patriarch and Prophets: Persecution of the Russian Orthodox Church, 132
"Pentecostals in Bulgaria," 228
"People and the Church Versus the State: The Case of the Roman Catholic Church in Poland," 325
People, Church and State in Modern Russia, 052
Persecuted but not Forsaken: The Story of the Church Behind

the Iron Curtain, 401
"Place of the Two Kingdom Doctrine in the Life of the Evangelical Churches in the German Democratic Republic," 258
Poland: Church Facing Socialism, 340
"Poland: in Mid 1984," 359
"Poland's Church on the Road to Gdansk," 350
"Polish Anxieties, Soviet Apprehensions," 343
"The Polish Church," 346
"The Polish Church and the Government,"336
"Polish Episcopate: Spokesman for Society,"322
"Polish Pope and the Polish Catholic Church,"330
"A Polish Strategy for Non-violent Change," 334
The Political, Social and Religious Thought of Russian Samizdat: An Anthology, 099
"Politics and Religion in Russia,"074
"Power in Church-State Relations in Eastern Europe," 039
Problems in Communism, 436
"Promise and Peril in Poland," 356
"Propaganda's Concern for the Church in Ukraine and Bielorussia," 168
"Protestantism in Czecho-slovakia," 244
Protestantism in Eastern Middle Europe, 047
"Protestantism in Hungary,"291
Protestants in Russia, 202

-R-

The Red Book of the Persecuted Church, 014
"Reductive Containment: Soviet Religious Policy," 076
"Reflections on the Role of the Catholic Church in Mediation the Present Crisis in Poland," 357
"Reform and Schism," 195
"The Reform Baptist Today," 211
"The Reformed Church in Hungary Today," 294
"Relations Between the State and the Roman Catholic Church in Croatia, Yugoslavia, in the 1970's and 1980's," 396
"Religion and Atheism in the USSR,"106
Religion and Communist Society, 012
"Religion and Human Rights: The Case of the Soviet Ukraine," 175
"Religion and Rights: A Dissenting Minority as a Social Movement in Romania," 367
"Religion and Soviet Youth," 095
Religion and Modernization in the Soviet Union, 070
"Religion and Nationalism in Lithuania," 189
"Religion and Nationalism in the USSR and China," 071
"Religion and Nationality in the Contemporary Ukraine," 170
"Religion and National Identity in Yugoslavia," 389
Religion and Soviet Foreign Policy 1945-1970, 077
"Religion and the Churches Function in Socialist Societies," 004
Religion and the Search for New Ideas in the USSR, 079
Religion and the Soviet State: A Dilemma of Power, 085
Religion Behind the Iron Curtain, 040
"Religion in a Communist Consumer Society: The Case of Kadar's Hungary," 301
Religion in Communist Countries: A Bibliography of Books in English, 048
Religion in Communist-Dominated Areas, 437
Religion in Communist Lands, 159, 438
Religion in Russia, 067
Religion in Russia Today, 055
"Religion in Soviet Marxist Societies: Ideology and Realpolitik," 033
Religion in Yugoslavia, 407
"Religion in Yugoslavia," 398
Religion in the Soviet Union, 060, 089
"Religion in the USSR," 111
Religion in the USSR, 069, 087

"Religion in the USSR After Khrushchev," 058
Religion Today in the Soviet Union, 100
"Religions and Churches Function in Socialist Societies," 034
The Religious and the Secular, 229
Religious and Anti-religious Thought in Russia, 088
"Religious Belief in the Brezhnev Era: Renaissance and Realpolitik," 091
Religious Change in Contemporary Poland: Secularization and Politics, 341
Religious Ferment in Russia: Protestant Opposition to Soviet Religious Policy, 196
Religious Freedom in Eastern Europe, 009
Religious Liberty in the Soviet Union: WCC and USSR--A Post Nairobi Documentation, 064
"Religious Liberty Under Communism," 001
Religious Life in Poland, 351
"The Religious-Non-Religious Dichotomy as a Social Problem," 312
"Religious Persecution in Albania," 225
Religious Persecution in the USSR, 090, 145
"Religious Problems in Russia Today," 112, 152
"Religious Protest Outcomes: The Soviet Baptist Case," 205
"Religious Renaissance in the Soviet Union," 072
"Religious Sectarianism and the Soviet State: The Dynamics of Believer Protest and Regime Response," 206
"Religious Situation in Czechoslovakia," 239
"The Religious Situation in the German Democratic Republic," 271
"Religious Values and Russian Political Dissent," 080
The Resistance of the Catholic Church in Lithuania Against Religious Persecution, 178
Return to Poland: The Collected Speeches of John Paul II, 329
"The Revolutionary Movement Against Religion in the Sixties," 222
Risen Indeed: Lessons in Faith from the USSR, 065
The Roman Catholic Church in Berlin and in the Soviet Zone of Germany, 266
"The Roman Catholic Church in Czechoslovakia," 243
"Romania's Churches Behind the Facade of Liberalism," 364
"Romanian Baptists and the State," 378
"The Romanian Orthodox Church," 372
The Romanian Orthodox Church, 373
Romanian Orthodox Church News: Fiftieth Anniversary of the Romanian Patriarchate, 375
"The Romanian Orthodox Church Today," 379
The Romanian Orthodox Church Yesterday and Today, 374
"Russia Tightens the Squeeze on Religious Dissidents," 056
Russian Church and the Soviet State, 1917-1950, 133
"The Russian Church, Religious Liberty and the World Council of Churches," 066
The Russian Church Under the Soviet Regime 1917-1982, 151
Russian Nonconformity: The Story of "Unofficial" Religion in Russia, 061
"The Russian Orthodox Church: 1945-1959," 146
"The Russian Orthodox Church, 1965-1980," 160
"The Russian Orthodox Church as Reflected in Orthodox and Atheist Publications in the Soviet Union," 142
The Russian Orthodox Church in the Fight for Peace: Decisions, Epistles, Appeals, and Articles, 1948-1950, 148, 154
The Russian Orthodox Church: Organization, Situation, Activity, 155, 156
The Russian Orthodox Church Underground, 1917-1970, 137
The Russian Protestants: Evangelicals in the Soviet Union: 1944-1964, 198

"Russian Religious Structures: A Study in Persistent Church Subservience," 101
The Russians and Their Church, 162
The Russians and the World Council, 139
Russia's Catacomb Saints, 129

-S-

"Secret Soviet Handbook on Religion," 118
Sects, Their Faith and Deeds, 199
Sermons in Solitary Confinement, 383
"The Shaping of Soviet Religious Policy," 059
"The Significance and Problems of Dialogue Today," 391
In Silence I Speak: The Story of Cardinal Mindsaenty Today and of Hungary's "New Order," 310
"The Sixth All-Christian Peace Assembly in 1985 in Prague: In Search of Peace and Justice for All," 416
"Social Change and Church Change," 098
Social Change in Soviet Russia, 086
"Social Class and Religion in Yugoslavia," 411
"The Socialist State and the Churches," 282
"Soft-Sell Ideology in Poland: Neither Churches nor State can Control the Outcome of the Country's Spreading Secularization," 331
"Some Characteristics of the Modern Baptist Movement," 207
"Some Explanations for the Persistance of Christian Religion in the Soviet Union," 094
"Some Social Expectations on Christians in Yugoslavia with Primary Emphasis on the Protestant Churches," 409
"Soviet Armenia and the Armenian Apostolic Church," 163
Soviet Believers: The Religious Sector of the Population, 078

"The Soviet Destruction of the Greek Catholic Church," 179
Soviet Evangelicals Since World War II, 212
"Soviet Evangelicals Today," 213
"Soviet Local Authorities Combat Religion (Moldavia SSR)," 053
"Soviet Lutheranism after the Second World War," 197
"Soviet Policy Towards Evangelicals," 210
"Soviet Religious Policy in the Ukraine in Historical Perspective," 171
The Soviet Saints, 217
"Soviet Weekly Attacks Four Churchmen," 115
Speeches on Peace: Third Series 1955-1957, 149
"Spotkania: Journal of the Catholic Opposition in Poland," 328
"State Authorities for Religious Affairs in Soviet Bloc Countries," 024
Statutes of the Christian Peace Conference, 417
"The Status of Cults," 116
"The Strengths of Weak Parties in the Church-State Confrontations: The Soviet Religion's Situations," 107
"The Study of Religion in Poland," 332
"The Study of Religion in the USSR [nauchnyy ateizm]," 125
Subversive Activities of the Evangelical Pastors in Bulgaria: Documents, 234
"Suffering from the Church? Aspects of Uneasiness at the Church Basis," 262
"A Summary of the Situation of the Hungarian Catholic Church," 309
Survey, 439
The Sword and the Ploughshare, 267
"Swords into Ploughshares: The Unofficial 'Peace Movement' and the Churches in East Germany," 252

-T-

Terror Over Yugoslavia: The Threat to Europe, 397

Theological Study in the Russian and Bulgarian Orthodox Churches under Communist Rule, 143
Theology Between Yesterday and Tomorrow, 238
"Theology of Liberation-- In the Spirit," 321
"Theses on the Role of the Church in the GDR," 278
Tortured for Christ, 384
Tortured for His Faith, 231
The Trial of Jozsef Mindszenty, 296
The Trial of the Fifteen Protestant Pastor-Spies, 233

-U-

"The Ukrainian Catholic Church, The Vatican and the Soviet Union during the Pontificate of Pope Paul II," 185
Ukrainian Churches Under Soviet Rule: Two Case Studies, 172
"The Understanding of Religious Freedom in the Socialist States," 025
"Urbanization, Operation Antireligion and the Decline of Religion in the USSR," 126
"USSR: The Christian Seminar," 136

-V-

Varieties of Christian-Marxist Dialogue, 032
The Vatican and Eastern Europe, 011
Visions Rise and Change, 104
A Voice in the Wilderness, 036, 153

-W-

The War Against God In Lithuania, 190
"We, Believers Do Not Want to Be Too Exacting," 405
"What is Published by the Catholic Press in Poland During the Period of Martial Law?," 319
White Paper on the Persecution of the Church in Poland, 354
"Who do you say I am," 251

With God in Russia, 068
"Working-Class Commitment to Religion and Society in Yugoslavia," 412

-Y-

"Yugoslavia: New Legislation on the Legal Staus of Religious Communities," 390

-Z-

"Zoltan Kaldy: A New Way for the Church in Socialism?," 292

Subject Index

This index includes subjects discussed in the Introductory Survey and in the Bibliographic Survey. References to the former are by page number; references to the latter are by the three-digit entry number; the two are separated by a semi-colon.

-A-

Anti-religious propaganda, pp. 20, 23; 053, 081, 087, 109, 126, 198-199, 204, 219-220, 222
Anti-religious thought, 088, 096, 124
Armenian Apostolic Church, 097, 163-166
Atheism and religion, pp. 20, 23, 25; 096, 106, 124-125, 142, 190, 219-220

-B-

Baptists in the USSR, pp. 7-8, 20; 105, 194-196, 198, 200-202, 204-214. See also Evangelical Baptists.
Base communities, 300
Bereczky, Albert, p. 10
Bibliographies, 048, 075
Bosnjak, Branko, p.23
Bulgarian Orthodox Church, pp. 7-9; 230, 233-234

-C-

Catholic lay organizations in Poland, p. 15; 330, 342
Catholic Press, p. 14; 319
Catholic University in Lublin, p. 15
Comprehensive treatment of the religious situation in the USSR and Eastern Europe, p. 8; 005, 018, 020, 043, 045, 069, 078, 082-084, 089, 093, 123, 151, 226-227, 240, 255, 270, 288, 340, 351, 386, 393
Christian Democratic Union, pp. 6, 15; 273
Christian Peace Conference, 414-419
Church of the Czech Bretheren, pp. 6, 10; 237-238, 241, 244-245, 250
Church-state reconciliation, 238, 241, 254, 256, 269, 279, 282-283, 286, 290, 292, 299, 313, 326, 360, 405
Church-state relations, in the USSR, pp. 4, 18-20;

Subject Index 107

003-004, 018-019, 039, 052, 069, 085-086, 092, 097, 105, 107, 111, 119, 133-134, 152, 158, 171-173, 210, 214
 in Albania, 218
 in Bulgaria, 227
 in Czechoslovakia, 236, 240-243
 in East Germany, 251, 254, 256-257, 270-272, 280-281
 in Hungary, 282-283, 285-286, 288, 290, 293, 295-296, 303-306, 310
 in Poland, 320, 325-327, 336, 350
 in Romania, 361, 370, 376, 378
 in Yugoslavia, 386-388, 394, 396, 400, 404
Ćimić, Esad, p. 23
Combating religion, 053, 069, 076, 210, 242, 246
Communist party, pp. 5, 19-20, 24
Communism, communists, pp. 4, 6-7, 11-13, 15, 20-22; 158, 232, 250
Constantinian model of church-state relations, pp. 3-4, 6
Councils for church affairs, pp. 22-23
Czechoslovak events, 1968, pp. 11, 14, 17, 21; 236, 241, 243

-D-

Dialogue between Christians and Marxists, p. 13;, 028-030, 032, 037, 241, 250, 284, 289-290, 323, 340, 391, 399, 410
Dissidents, dissent, pp. 7-9, 25; 015, 049-050, 056, 061, 080, 099, 113, 119, 127-128, 132, 135-137, 140-141, 146, 153, 157, 174, 178, 183, 185, 192-196, 198, 200, 204-206, 212, 214, 300, 328, 340, 367, 377

-E-

Eastern Orthodox Churches, p.7. See also Bulgarian, Romanian, and Russian Orthodox Church.
Ecumenism, 139, 147, 152, 161, 237, 245, 340, 371

Evangelical Baptists, pp.7; 194-196, 198-203, 207, 210. See also Baptists in the USSR.
Evangelical Lutheran Churches in East Germany, pp. 9; 251, 254, 268, 270, 272, 276, 279, 281

-F-

Family and the Church, 086
Foreign policy and religion, 077
"Free Churches," p. 4
Frid, Zlatko, p. 23

-G-

Gardavský, Vítězslav, p. 23
Georgian Orthodox Church, p. 16; 097, 167

-H-

Hromádka, Joseph, pp. 6, 10; 238, 241, 244, 250
Hungarian Lutheran Church, pp. 6, 10; 292, 308, 314-315
Hungarian Reformed Church, pp. 6, 8, 10; 293-294, 313
Hungarian Revolt, 1956, pp. 10-11, 17
Human rights and religion, pp. 13, 25; 128, 135, 175, 178, 337

-I-

Influence of churches on society, pp. 3-17; 012-013, 016, 070, 073
Influence of society on churches, pp. 19-26

-J-

Jaruzelski, General, p. 22
John Paul II (Karol Wojtiła), 329-330, 349-350, 352, 358

-K-

Kadar regime, p. 6
Kadlecova, Erika, p. 23
Káldy, Zóltan, 292
Kerševan, Marko, p. 23
Krešić, Andrija, p. 23
Kuczyński, Janusz, p. 23

-L-

Laws regarding religion, p. 20; 003, 018, 024, 041, 043, 045, 064, 116-118, 122, 158, 226, 240, 242, 288, 390, 393, 405, 408
Life-Light Movement, 321, 333-334
Lukács, József, p. 23
Luther, Martin, 253, 256, 261

-M-

Machovec, Milan, p. 23
Marxism, Marxists, pp. 5, 11-13, 18-19, 21, 23-24; 241, 254, 256, 302, 399, 400
Mennonites in the USSR, p. 4; 215-216
Mihajlov, Mihajlo, p. 14
Mindszenty, József, p. 6; 296, 304-306, 310, 316
Modernization and religion, 070
Monasticism, 369
Moral and ethical impact of religion, pp. 12-13; 166, 241, 289

-N-

Nationalism and religion, p. 12; 034, 071, 085, 110, 166, 170, 189, 192-193, 203, 318, 347, 357, 360, 366, 389
Non-violent change, 193, 334

-P-

Peacemaking of churches, pp. 13; 139, 147-149, 154, 158, 161, 243, 248, 252, 263-264, 267, 414-419
Pentecostals in Bulgaria, 228
Persecution of religion, p. 5; 014, 017, 020, 026-027, 040, 062-063, 065, 067-068, 084, 087, 090, 103, 115, 129, 131-132, 136-138, 145-146, 153, 159, 168-169, 174, 178, 184-187, 190-191, 200, 212, 217, 219-220, 223-225, 230-231, 233-234, 293, 304-306, 310, 344, 354, 380-385, 392, 397, 401
Persistence of religion, 094, 104, 111, 130, 137, 193, 312
Péter, János, p. 8

Polish Catholic Episcopate, p. 12; 322
Polish events, 1980s, pp. 11, 17; 325, 350, 356-357
Polish United Worker's Party, p. 22
Politics and religion, 074, 077, 085, 139, 160, 235
Popoff, Haralan, p. 8
Pospieluszko, Jerzy, p. 14; 344
Protestants, pp. 4, 6, 8-9, 12; 047, 194-217, 228, 230-231, 233-234, 236-238, 251, 256-261, 268, 272, 274, 276, 279-281, 291-294, 298, 313-315, 359, 368, 378, 401, 409

-R-

Reform Evangelical Baptists in the USSR, p. 7; 194-196, 198, 211
Religion
 in Albania, 218-225
 in Bulgaria, 226-234
 in Czechoslovakia, 235-250
 in East Germany, 251-281
 in Hungary, 282-316
 in Poland, 317-360
 in Romania, 361-385
 in the USSR, 051-217
 in Yugoslavia, 386-413
Religion reflected in literature, 051, 111
Religious liberty, pp. 18, 25; 001, 009, 025, 064, 066, 092, 120, 128, 174, 178, 182, 202, 338, 394
Resurgence of religion, p. 16; 063, 072, 078, 091, 095, 160, 196, 247, 318, 341, 351, 392
Roman Catholic Church, pp. 4, 12-13, 17; 168-193, 242-243, 246, 248-249
 in Croatia, p. 12; 396, 406
 in Czechoslovakia, pp. 8, 21; 235, 242-243, 246-248
 in East Germany, 266
 in Hungary, pp. 6, 8; 283, 286-287, 295-297, 301, 305-306, 309-310
 in Lithuania, p. 8; 174, 176, 178, 183, 189-193
 in Poland, pp. 5, 11, 15, 22; 322, 325, 330, 335-336, 346, 348, 350, 355, 357, 360
 in Romania, 362-363

in Ukraine, p. 20; 168-169, 172-173
in Yugoslavia, p. 12; 396, 405-406
Romanian Orthodox Church, pp. 20-21; 366, 372-375, 379
Roter, Zdenko, p. 23; 037
Rural population and religion, 073
Russian Orthodox Church, pp. 4-5, 7, 17, 19-20; 100, 105, 129-162

-S-

Secularization and religion, pp. 16, 24; 035, 078-079, 126, 229, 311-312, 331, 339, 341
Social change and religion, 086, 098, 339
Social class and religion, p. 24; 411-412
"Socialist religion." p. 10
Socialist Unity Party of GDR, pp. 6, 15, 21
"Solidarity" labor union, pp. 5, 11-12, 15, 24; 343-344, 350, 356
Solzhenitsyn, Alexander, p. 14; 157
Soviet religious policy, 059, 076-077, 087, 100, 108, 114, 117-118, 131, 146, 150, 155-157, 162, 171-172
Stepinac, Alojzije, p. 16; 386, 402-403, 413

-T-

Theological studies, 143
"Theology of diaconia," p. 6; 292, 308, 314-315
Theology of liberation, 322

-U-

Ukrainian Orthodox question, 153, 159
Urbanization and religion, 126, 339

-V-

Vatican and Communism, p. 17; 007, 011, 042
Vinns, Georgiy, p. 8
Violations of religious liberty, 062, 064, 066, 182, 242, 249. See also persecution of religion.
Vrcan, Srdjan, p. 23; 411-412

-W-

Wurmbrand, Richard, p. 8; 380-384

-Y-

Youth and religion, p. 11; 095, 300, 333
Yugoslav socialism, p. 22; 406

About the Compiler

PAUL MOJZES is Professor of Religious Studies at Rosemont College, Rosemont, Pennsylvania. He is the author of *Christian-Marxist Dialogue in Eastern Europe* and the editor of *Varieties of Christian-Marxist Dialogue* and *Society and Original Sin*.